D0899264

A
GLIMPSE
OF
EMPIRE

A
GLIMPSE
OF
EMPIRE

——

JESSICA
DOUGLAS-HOME

MICHAEL RUSSELL

First published in Great Britain 2011
by Michael Russell (Publishing) Ltd
Wilby Hall, Wilby, Norwich NR16 2JP

Page makeup in Sabon by Waveney Typesetters
Wymondham, Norfolk
Printed in Great Britain by the MPG Books Group
Bodmin and King's Lynn

ISBN 978-0-85955-321-6

TO LILAH'S GREAT-GREAT-GRANDCHILDREN
NICHOLAS, SELINA, LILAH AND GABRIEL
WHO LOVE HER NORFOLK HOUSE TO THIS DAY

Contents

LILAH'S INDIAN JOURNEY
NOVEMBER 1911 ~ FEBRUARY 1912

AFGHANISTAN

Peshawar
Rawalpindi

TIBET

NEPAL

Delhi

Jaipur

Lucknow

Agra
Cawnpore

Udaipur

Benares

Bhopal

Calcutta

INDIA

Bombay

S.S Malwja

Bangalore

S.S Malwa

Colombo

THE MAHARAJAS' CAMPS
IN
THE TENTED CITY

Durbar Amphitheatre

King's Way

Puna's Road

Rutram

Sikkim Bhutan

Market

Jaipur

Nawanagar

Jodhpur

police

Bikener

Kashmir

Bhopal

Kingsway Station

Menar

Indore

Baroda

Patiala

Foreign Office

Hyderabad

Mysore

The Mall

The Ridge

Polo Ground

H.E. The Viceroy

Dairy

Grand Trunk Road

H.I.M. The King-Emperor

Veterans Camp

Veterinary Hospital

Imperial Government

Flagstaff Tower

Acknowledgements

I thank my cousins Carey Basset and Anne Tennant for discovering Lilah's diary. I am especially grateful too for the help on my text from Nawshir Mirza. From him, and also from Lakshman Menon, I learnt so much about India.

Benjamin Buchan, Agnieszka Kolakowska and Roger Scruton have helped me by supplying important insights, looking at the text and correcting errors. There have been many more who, through their patience in answering questions on historical detail, have helped me more than they would know. I thank David Airlie, John Ashburton, Crispin Bates, David Campbell, Anne de Courcy, my brother Martin Gwynne, Lord Iveagh, Amin Jaffer, the Maharaja of Jodhpur, Amabel Lindsay, Le Comte Jean de Madre, Anthony Mildmay-White, Christian Moxon, Francis Russell, Jonathan Scott, Shubhanginiraje Gaekwad, Xan Smiley, Cindy Shaw-Stewart, Roddy Sale and Lord Willoughby de Broke.

I would also like to thank everyone who works at the London Library, the British Library, the Holkham Estate archives, the Cambridge University Library, the Royal Archives at Windsor and the Museum of the King's Royal Hussars.

For much help with photographs I thank Derry Moore, Jossy Dimbleby and Sandra Rosignioli — and of course Maggie Evans and David Mallinson.

I must thank Rachel Saunders for her optimistic and undaunted attitude to typing and re-typing my constant revisions and for her research.

To give thanks to a husband at the end of acknowledgements often seems a cliché. Whatever the case, I owe everything to my husband, Rodney Leach, for the help he has given me in completing this book: his meticulous care in discussing detail, improvements and revision, his moral support and his laughter.

[xi]

Preface

The first time I ransacked my grandmother Lilah's red leather and gold photograph albums for information was when I was a young theatre designer at the National Theatre. Having gleaned all I could from them about Victorian costumes for a production of J. B. Priestley's *When We Are Married*, I inadvertently left one album in the theatre. When I retrieved it the next morning, it was covered in coffee stains and chocolate smears from the late-night attentions of stage hands and seamstresses.

Looking at them again thirty years later, I have treated her albums with more respect. The quality of her small photographs is not obvious to an amateur and I might not have recognised it but for the photographer David Mallinson and the art historian Maggie Evans. For the discovery of Lilah's diary I have to thank the initiative of a total stranger who discovered it in a second hand bookshop in Norfolk in 1999 and decided to track down her relatives. We have no idea how it reached the shop. To marry the photographs with the diary was to transform the interest of both, and has been the greatest of pleasures.

Lilah's tale is that of a courageous young woman who, but for her Irish upbringing, would probably have conformed to the claustrophobic Edwardian and aristocratic conventions of her gloomy elderly mother. To escape and find herself, she set off for India in 1911 to attend King George V's Coronation Durbar. It was the apogee of the British Empire, and the celebration was on an unimaginably grand scale, but what Lilah fell in love with there was not so much Britain in India as India itself.

I

Childhood in Ireland

In 1911, the year of which I write, my Irish grandmother Lilah Wingfield was a beautiful young woman of twenty-three. Nearly six foot tall, with deep-set brown eyes in a classically proportioned face, she had rich, auburn hair, a full bosom and a tiny waist. Extrovert, imaginative and artistic, she was passionate in conversation and possessed a flow of vital energy by which in later years, even when she was in her nineties, our family was frequently overwhelmed. My brother adored her. We would sit at her feet listening to her in her Norfolk sitting room as, majestically upright in her winged arm chair, she told us of her complicated emotional life before the First World War.

Lilah's mother, Julia, was quintessentially English, brought up by her father, the Earl of Leicester, in Victorian patrician style. Their life was divided between an elegant London house and a large country estate – Holkham Hall, the magnificent eighteenth-century house (still in the family) on the North Norfolk coast, a mile from the dunes and pine woods, marshes, creeks and mud flats by the sea, with their great open skies of wild geese and gulls' cries. In 1864, when Julia was twenty, her father had invited a friend to shoot and had told her this was the man she was to marry. Six months later she departed – obedient, wedded and homesick – to Ireland.

The selected husband was Mervyn Wingfield, the 7th Viscount Powerscourt. As a child Mervyn had inherited land stretching over several counties. At the foot of the Wicklow Mountains and dating from the thirteenth century, Powerscourt Castle and its gardens had been rebuilt and refashioned by generations of Wingfields. In 1857, at the age of twenty-one, Mervyn too had embarked on an ambitious plan of improvements, which were to take him twenty years to complete. By the time Lilah was born thirty-one years later, he had turned the place into a majestic Palladian-style house, from which he travelled to Dublin every week to preside over museums, art galleries and hospitals.

During the first sixteen years of marriage Julia was childless, lonely and a little unsettled by the violent undercurrent of Republicanism which was then disturbing the superficial tranquillity of Ireland. She constantly travelled back to England, which for her remained home. And then after sixteen years of marriage, she produced five children in quick succession. Lilah was the youngest.

Lilah's parents were remote figures who lived and entertained, surrounded by servants, in a different part of the house from the place where the children were kept. Lilah slept with the nanny in the night nursery, with no heating, no open fire, no eiderdowns and not even hot water bottles. Children were meant to be impervious to cold. Lilah recalled:

Nanny put her flannel apron on the bed to warm our frozen feet. We lived simple lives with rarely any treats or excitements. Yet we were amazingly happy – playing invented games, wrapped in our own world, in corridors and attics or among the trees in the woods round the house. After tea we would dress to visit our parents in our party frocks, with wide silk sashes and embroidered bronze-coloured stockings and shoes. The drawing room was several minutes away. To reach it, we covered up in shawls to survive the freezing passages. Once there, mercifully always finding a huge open fire, we were meant to supply our own occupation until the longed for moment came when we could rush back to the nursery. We always had the same supper – a glass of milk, a slice of bread and butter. Nothing more in this monotonous diet was ever given us. No fruit, no biscuits and no sweets.

Each morning, during the break in lessons, the children had five minutes to change into riding habits and get to the stables, where they were helped to mount by the head coachman. They were accompanied on this formal ride by a groom in the Powerscourt livery. Then a quick change and back to the schoolroom. Later in the day they were left to their own devices, tending their pets – birds, rabbits, guinea pigs and beloved dogs – or roaming the 50,000 acres of parkland, free at last to ride bareback or to harness their Iceland ponies onto a little wooden two-wheeled cart. They drove at breakneck speed down the Wicklow hills, once causing Lilah to shoot out over the cart onto her head on the stony road. She awoke with a terrible headache to find her brother Maurice pouring whiskey down her throat. Such events were never relayed to the grown-ups.

Sometimes the children would fish or go swimming in the lake or picnic at the foot of the Great Sugar Loaf mountain and climb by the Powerscourt waterfall, the highest in Ireland, which cascades 400 feet into the valley below. Once a week, with their 1d pocket money for sweets, they drove their open wagonette to the village shop in Enniskerry. If, as sometimes happened, they were invited to the houses of the local gentry, that would have meant travelling further and taking the Powerscourt landau or brougham, which were forbidden them. Anyway, they had company enough – their best friends were the little daughter of the head gardener and the children of the gamekeeper and the head steward.

Lilah's four English aunts – all but one of whom, obedient to their parents' instructions, had married into noble estates – visited Powers-court at regular intervals to berate Julia over the behaviour of her children. Lilah writes:

> We were utterly in awe of the aunts. Whenever one of them came to stay we had to be on our best behaviour. It was a great strain. They all disapproved of us and my mother listened to them, worrying over their criticisms of our wild Irish ways. She always tried to reform us after they had left. Aunt Mary particularly scared us. She was very Victorian, an absolute ruler in her own family. My mother was putty in her hands. Aunt Mary was very conscious of her position as one of London's leading hostesses, and was determined that my mother should not let the side down.

Eventually, Lilah's brothers went to boarding school in England, leaving Lilah and her two sisters to be taught by a series of unloved German and French governesses. Such adult affection as she received came from her adored, very religious nanny who was employed by the family for twenty-one years, not leaving until Lilah was fourteen.

> Nanny taught me all I ever learned of good behaviour and manners and the reasons for it. She looked after our well-being and made all our clothes. I don't remember my mother ever

[4]

coming into the nursery, ever reading to us or playing with us. We used to appear briefly for 'the children's hour' of an evening – counting the minutes until we could return to Nanny. Yet I loved my mother very much and still recall the feeling of loss when she departed on her visits to England, leaving us behind with my father.

The possession of a young Irish family did nothing to improve Julia's affection for Ireland. She frequently abandoned her daughters and her husband in Powerscourt, even for Christmas, taking her two sons on their own to Holkham. The family summer house-party, however, following the London season spent by the parents in their house in Brook Street, was sacrosanct. This annual exodus to Norfolk involved massive logistical preparation. The Powerscourt housekeeper, a stiff, grand and alarming woman with a starched lace bonnet, took charge. She marshalled the conveying of the eleven servants (all of whom she had engaged herself), the horses and carriages, even the nanny, with her trunks full of toys and clothes. The first group left on the thirteen-hour journey to England a week in advance, the Wingfield children a little later. They went five miles by carriage to Bray and on by train to Kingston pier (now Dun Laoghaire) to catch the antiquated Irish Mail steamer, where they were made to lie down in the ladies' salon. After the often rough crossing and sea-sickness, they would arrive in the middle of the night at Holyhead, where they got into a second-class carriage of the London train. The nanny lay on one side of their carriage with the girls lying feet to feet on the other side and the boys on a rug on the floor. The nurserymaids sat outside in the corridor. Six hours later they would step off at Euston half dead with fatigue, the experience made worse by their nanny's belief in forestalling the rigours of the journey by making each of them take a dose of the mysterious Gregory's Powder the night before. It was supposed to settle the stomach before the ordeal, but it had the opposite effect.

Lilah hated leaving Powerscourt: '... just at the loveliest time of year, even for a few weeks. I remember visiting all our favourite places and saying a tearful goodbye to our animals. My sister Olive once gave the wall of the house a lingering kiss, and none of us thought this strange or sentimental.'

The wild and intensely happy Irish way of life came abruptly to an end with the death of Lilah's father from pneumonia in 1904. She was sixteen. His illness was sudden and shattering. In her nursery days, they had been like strangers, but over the last two years their relationship had begun to flourish. He took her to shooting and tennis parties, polo matches, tea with the Viceroy in Dublin. These leisurely journeys in his landau gave them ample opportunity to get to know each other. Now, before their growing affection had had time to mature, he was taken from her.

Her paradoxical attitude to empire was formed in her adolescence. She had grown up in a divided country, riven by vast discrepancies of wealth and poverty, by the grievances of disenfranchised Catholics and the sectarian violence of Ireland's mutinous tenant farmers. She felt herself Irish to the core, but at the same time she was Protestant and insulated from much of the bitterness by her father's popularity as an enlightened landlord. A child of her background, she believed as instinctively in the inherited English political and social order as in the natural rights of the Irish. If that was inconsistent, so was much else in Britain's paternalist, often idealistic, view of its Empire.

The Wingfields had lived in Powerscourt for four centuries. Close to Dublin, its beauty was a magnet for the landed Irish gentry and visiting grandees. While her mother looked on Ireland as a colonial outpost, for Lilah, Dublin Castle, with its viceregal splendour, was the axis of the society she knew. Its rituals were to her as enduring as life itself – the pageantry, the investitures, parades, levees and royal celebrations; and alongside the State events, the balls, the summer entertainments, then in winter the hunting. In her eyes, Dublin and London were co-equals. If she thought of herself as colonial, that was without the slightest sense of inferiority towards the mother country. Years later, when she went to India, it was with a total absence of the condescension with which so many of the English regarded their most exotic colony.

As the days of her father's funeral drew near, it quickly dawned on her that, in losing him, she had lost her beloved home. The new Viscount, her recently married brother, moved into Powerscourt with indecent haste. Her mother bought a new London house in Harley Street. Here she settled with Lilah and her remaining children.

The departure had been abrupt and complete. All Lilah's pets were disposed of, her pony, Shamrock, given away and her pug housed with a gatekeeper. She recollected:

I was not old enough to imagine any substitute for the life I had lived in Ireland. I had to exchange my freedom for the ordered lives of English girls, of whose restrictions and priorities I knew nothing. I deeply resented the change and took a long time to get broken in to it. How I hated leaving Ireland!

To make matters worse, she was deserted by her two older sisters during their 'coming out', when they were chaperoned through the London Season by their aunts, who missed no opportunity to criticise their unsophisticated Irish manners. Aunt Mary (the haughty Lady Dartmouth) took it on herself to issue a solemn warning that Julia's foolish move to Harley Street had ruined the prospects of her daughters, who would now meet nobody but doctors.

If Lilah's independent character never failed to shock her mother and her aunts, young men were captivated by her love of life, her flirtatiousness and her rebellious streak. Her admirers were not always suitable financially – a further source of family disapproval. By 1910 she had found it so difficult to sustain normal friendships with men that she felt she had to give the matter serious thought. Most of her female friends had married after their first Season. Her own presentation at Court was now four years behind her, but she was not susceptible to the conventional type of suitor her mother and her aunts encouraged her to meet and she had no intention of marrying just for the sake of it. The rigid customs of her upbringing forbade the prospect of a profession, and she was not cut out to be the companion for life that her increasingly demanding seventy-year old mother wanted. Harry MacGeagh, the one man whom she allowed to kiss her and whose company she really enjoyed, was not quite someone she wanted to spend her life with. Nor was he rich enough to be one of those compromise husbands that Edwardian ladies often settled for.

Things came to a head in the summer of 1910. Her favourite sister, Clare, her only still unmarried sibling, was allowed to go to Powerscourt to stay with her brother and enjoy Dublin's festivities for the whole of August. Lilah, said her mother, would not be going. She would be spending the summer with her in a rented rectory in Cromer, after which they would finish the holiday at Holkham: 'I did my utmost to persuade Mother to let me go to Ireland but it was no good... Life is getting unbearable nowadays through her not letting me *any* independence; I shall have to break out and fight for my freedom soon, if this goes on much longer. If only she *knew* how much she is alienating all my affection for her by her injustice to me.'

After a depressing month in Cromer, they joined the rest of the family at Holkham. The old Lord Leicester had recently died and had been succeeded by Julia's brother Richard. The vast house, a mile in circumference, had been much in need of modernisation – a massive undertaking which Richard had to tackle as soon as he inherited. By the end of 1910 he had installed electricity and made enough progress to be able to invite the usual September house party of some fifty friends and relations.

A letter written by a distant cousin says a lot about how Lilah was seen at the time by her contemporaries:

> This afternoon on the sand hills Ned, Lilah Wingfield and I gravely discussed the pros and cons of getting married, Mabel occasionally joining in and treating the subject like the buying of a tiresome piece of furniture. 'Oh of course I call it a lottery' said Ned in his cheerful voice, and Lilah Wingfield agreed, adding that no girl should marry until 28, and then to a man of nearly 40. 'That's too old' objected Mabel. 'They are the only ones worth talking to' replied Lilah, flashing her fine eyes. She is a great personality, Lilah – it will be interesting to see what she makes of her life. Lady Powerscourt is non-plussed by her, and is shocked by her frank careless remarks every minute: at luncheon today she said 'Oh Mother, did I tell you of the man at the Inchiquins' ball, who asked me if Lady Inchiquin drank?' – 'Yes you did, it was a question that could not have been asked by any gentleman, and the answer you gave was totally unnecessary.' 'That she took morphia? Well, it was true.'

Lilah complained to her cousin that the aunts had no sense of humour and had knocked it out of Julia. 'I told Mother one day that I liked "Bad Hats". She was miserable and thought it a very serious failing in my character.'

[8]

News now of Clare's engagement came as an appalling blow to Lilah. She adored her sister and was very happy for her, but her marriage would leave Lilah alone in Harley Street with her selfish, controlling mother without any confidante to soothe her wounds and ease her sense of bitterness. Escape was the only answer. She would travel – to Rome, to America, to the East, anywhere to get away from the oppressive presence of her mother.

It was a sad Christmas, made sadder by Clare's imminent departure. However, the death of King Edward VII and the accession of George V brought her an unexpected opportunity. A whole-page advertisement in the *Illustrated London News* in the spring of 1911 carried the schedule of a train company serving the Royal Durbar in Delhi later in the year. There was a sketch of an elephant decked in gold emblems with a howdah and a jewelled canopy. The text read: 'To those who have leisure, no more delightful route to India could be suggested, through picturesque Rockies, Japan and China on the Canadian Pacific Railway, leaving London in September.'

Lilah would need a convincing advocate with her mother if she was to be allowed the wild folly of an expedition to the Orient. She wrote to Judy Smith, a middle-aged friend and distant relative of the family, to enlist her support. Together they concocted their story. Lilah ought to get married but was bored by her admirers in London. She needed somebody at once more adventurous and more suitable – the sort of person, in a word, who might be part of the royal entourage to the Durbar. Between these four walls, Judy would add, Lilah is quite close to nervous collapse – and it was vital to separate her from her lingering affection for Harry MacGeagh. After an agonising pause Julia gave her permission.

Lilah promptly contacted her closest friend in Ireland, Sylvia Brooke, and began making plans.

2

Preparing for India

From the moment of his accession in 1910, George V was determined to travel to Delhi to have himself crowned Emperor of India. Queen Victoria's Royal Durbar in 1877, the brainchild of Disraeli, had been a political celebration of her proclamation as Empress of India, a demonstration of Britain's imperial power. But the Queen herself had not crossed the seas. The 1903 Durbar to mark King Edward VII's accession had been notably more extravagant, but he too had left the conduct of the ceremony to his Viceroy, Lord Curzon. The Durbar – the holding of a court audience – owed its origins to ancient Mughal conventions at which the feudal ruler would receive visitors, confer honours and conduct business. To this the maharajas had added their own pageantry and symbolic display. The Royal Durbar was a British invention, in which the spectacle of the Indian princes paying homage to the Crown was further enhanced by an impressive parade of the might of the Imperial Army.

In 1910 there were new strategic factors to be considered, chief among them fresh ripples of unrest against British rule in India and a tense industrial scene at home. The Government accepted that a coronation in Delhi, if masterminded with suitable magnificence, could reinforce the loyalty of the princes and arouse the enthusiasm of the whole country. King George went further. He had been captivated by that 'fascinating and multitudinous country' when he had visited it as Prince of Wales on the occasion of Lord Curzon's Durbar seven years earlier. He told the Secretary of State that he wished 'no longer to be a vague and remote personage to my Indian subjects in that vast land, ruling from a remote far-off island in the northern seas'.

Against the King's determination to go, many cautious voices were raised. The proposal was discussed at length in Prime Minister Asquith's Liberal cabinet during the autumn of 1910. It was unprecedented that a reigning monarch be absent from England for so long. There was trouble enough at home, with strikes, lockouts and radicalism on the increase and the growing influence of the firebrand David Lloyd George, who made the impressionable Lilah feel she was participating in 'something like the French Revolution'. The bloody Indian Mutiny of 1857 was hardly distant history. How could royal protection from assassins be ensured? And who would pay for it all? Memories still rankled of the colossal cost of Lord Curzon's Durbar. What honours and hand-outs should be offered to the princes? How would the Government cover the King's absence for so protracted a period, with a long sea voyage intervening? The Archbishop of Canterbury joined the debate, objecting to a second Christian service of consecration on the grounds that it would be unfitting in the presence of a population so far outnumbered by Muslims and Hindus. He also pointed out that English law did not permit the Crown to leave the kingdom.

Finally, after many compromises and modifications, a plan was accepted. A Durbar Committee was appointed by the Viceroy Lord Hardinge to be chaired by Sir John Hewett, an experienced Indian administrator. Time was short. Five months after his June coronation at Westminster Abbey, the King with his wife Queen Mary would travel to India by boat. A new 13,000-ton vessel, the *Medina*, was requisitioned from P&O and an ambitious scheme of interior decoration set in motion. The royal suite was furnished in satinwood and green upholstery. Queen Mary, a poor sailor, had a special swinging cot designed for her, in case of rough weather.

On 3 November 1911 the King (the first English king to leave Europe since Richard Coeur de Lion) set sail from Marseilles. The ship was escorted by four cruisers and had on board 733 souls, including the Secretary of State for India Lord Crewe, the Chief of the Metropolitan Police, political secretaries, a royal librarian, a protective squadron of Royal Marines and various personal friends. Three cows from Windsor had been lowered into the ship by pulley and were expected to produce fresh milk daily. The journey to India would last three weeks, interrupted briefly for official meetings in Gibraltar, Suez and Aden.

Known only to the innermost circle of the politically trustworthy, the King and Lord Crewe carried in their papers an announcement to be made to the Indian people at the Durbar ceremony – a secret so sensitive that it was not even shared with the Queen.

As for Lilah, conventional social life of ever-diminishing interest filled the interlude before her journey, relieved only by Easter at Holkham and a stay with her brother at Powerscourt. Her chief purpose in going to Ireland was to finalise plans with her future travelling companion Sylvia Brooke, 'just as beautiful as Lilah, but less of a handful' as Mervyn put it. They would, of course, need a chaperone, but fortunately Judy Smith herself was game for the adventure. Ten years older than Lilah and recently widowed, she would fit the bill perfectly. A male escort would also come in handy, especially one with useful experience. As her first choice Julia lit on Arthur Brodrick, a safe and very competent middle-aged family friend with extensive connections in the Army and the Indian Civil Service. He was more than happy to accompany two attractive young women for the best part of three months. They were equally happy to accept him, and the party was now complete.

After Ireland came another London season, where she received more proposals and indulged in some harmless flirtations with two of her extended family. But it was all unsatisfying and when the Irish-German Prince and Princess Alexander of Teck, who leased the Home Farm at Holkham, invited her to a fancy dress ball at the Savoy Hotel, she made a gesture of identity, going as an Irish peasant colleen. (She was trumped by the illustrious ballerina Anna Pavlova, who with a fine sense of her own genius went as herself.)

The Festival of Empire exhibition was already in full swing at the Crystal Palace in south London, its twenty sites reachable by travelling one and a half miles on a small train which stopped at every stand. Lilah picked up Sylvia and together they made for the central square, descending at the ornate domed Indian Building. Here they experienced their first taste of a bazaar and were introduced to the tall and elegant twenty-year-old Maharaja Holkar of Indore, who chanced to be visiting the exhibition with his exotic retinue.

It was standard Foreign Office practice to encourage the leading Indian princes to visit England and attend public occasions in the hope that this would inspire them to emulate British standards of governance. (Not every prince, it should be said, was considered the right material for absorbing such lessons – the unreliable Raja Bhairava Tondiman of Pudukota had applied to attend Queen Victoria's Jubilee in 1897 but had been refused on the pretext that he could not afford it.) Much hope was invested in the young Maharaja of Indore by the Indian Government, in whose eyes his father, who had been forced to abdicate in 1903, was a despot mired in oriental excess. For the last seven years, contact between father and son had been strictly controlled by the Viceroy, who had packed the son off to the right Indian Imperial colleges. His best achievement at the Mayo College had been to stand first in the ancient game of tent pegging – a military exercise to hone a galloping rider's skill at stabbing elephants' toes. He finally joined the Imperial Cadet Corps, where he developed a 'fever' and did not complete his course, an early warning that he might have inherited more than a title from his father.

The Maharaja had been in the royal box for the opening of the Crystal Palace Festival in May, and was to be in the royal family's innermost circle again for King George's Coronation. More significantly, he had been chosen to unveil the plaque in St Paul's to Sir Curzon Wyllie, a senior British Indian Government official who had been assassinated in London two years earlier. The assassin, Madan Lal Dhingra, had been hanged, at once becoming a martyr of the Indian independence movement.

Lilah immersed herself in books on India. Lovat Fraser's biography *India under Lord Curzon and After* tried her powers of endurance. More to her liking were the tales and ballads of Rudyard Kipling and the novels of Maud Diver about military life on the North-West Frontier. Kipling gave her a feel for the real India – of caste, of ordinary British soldiers and of superstition, teeming cities and untamed nature. Diver's trilogy swept her up into a world of tall, intrepid, gentle-hearted captains in constant danger from hostile tribesmen, trapped in the camps with silly wives (from whom they would be mercifully released by consumption or assassination) or saved from sin or morphia addiction by some impeccable visiting beauty. But not all Lilah's reading consisted of page-turners. The Book of the Month that September was *Letters from India* by Lady Wilson, whose husband had been in the Indian Civil Service. Lady Wilson castigated her sister British memsahibs for not questioning the Indian practice of purdah. 'Most [British] women resident in India ignored the very existence of Indian women of every class ... beautifully bejewelled beings

[13]

... whether the wives of the village headman, artisans, peasants...' Her own proudest achievement was to have established medical schools for Indian women doctors in four cities.

Lilah's gold-embossed invitation to the Durbar arrived in September. She and Sylvia, whose brother Basil was in the 10th Hussars, would stay under the protection of his regiment, as would Judy Smith. Arthur Brodrick would make his own arrangements with the India Office. At first Lilah was reluctant to travel all the way by sea: it was such a long voyage and she remembered many rough crossings from Ireland. She also had a horror of rats. She had been alarmed recently to read of ships coming into London carrying Manchurian mountain rats which ran up and down the mooring ropes in the London Docks, treating them as a highway and spreading the plague bacilli onto dry land.

But her brother Mervyn persuaded her that a good liner – sailing from Marseilles to avoid the treacherous weather of the Bay of Biscay – was a better plan. To accommodate the numbers of peers attending the Durbar, the organising Committee had chartered a new vessel, the *Maloja*, sister ship to the royal party's *Medina*. Under recently introduced by-laws, said Mervyn, the master of any passenger steamer who had not fitted anti-rodent protection would be heavily fined. A modern vessel like the *Maloja* would certainly be equipped with elaborate fumigating pumps to discharge sulphur dioxide through pipes into the hold and exterminate the rats.

At eleven on the morning of 13 November 1911, Lilah and her three companions waved goodbye in Victoria Station to a crowd of friends who had turned up to wish them well. Lilah survived a very rough crossing from Dover to Calais without being seasick, and at 7 a.m. the next morning she stepped from the Calais night train onto the Marseilles quay. Their liner was waiting alongside, with passengers already aboard. The *Maloja*'s maiden voyage had started a week earlier at Tilbury.

3
On Board the Maloja

The ship's size gave Lilah confidence. It should be a smooth passage whatever the weather. At 569 feet in length *Maloja* was the largest vessel yet built for the P&O – the pride of the fleet, a passenger and mail ship of the highest class. It claimed the latest improvements in construction and design, with accommodation for 670 passengers (20 more than the *Medina*) and wireless telegraphy and electricity throughout.

Lilah shared a cabin suite with Sylvia. Judy had one on the upper deck and Arthur Brodrick had one even higher. After bathing and breakfasting, Lilah began to survey her fellow passengers. There was a strong Irish contingent revolving round the elderly Lord Iveagh, a friend and neighbour of her father. The Shaw-Stewarts and Lord and Lady Bute (who lived a stone's throw from each other on the Isle of Bute) had assumed social leadership of the Scottish group, whose other notables included the Duke and Duchess of Hamilton and the Earl and Countess of Mar and Kellie (the Earl was to have a quasi-official position at the Durbar representing the Royal Company of Archers as the King's Scottish bodyguard – the first time the Archers had served abroad).

Then there was the Comte de Madre: 'Arthur introduced me to a funny old Frenchman who thought himself quite the gay dog.' Clearly proud of his looks, he liked to strike an impressive pose, 'right foot slightly forward, left hand on hip'. However, much more intriguing to Lilah were two Indians, 'one of whom was quite a little boy, the Maharaja of Jodhpur ... and in his suite Thakur Dhokal Singh, a most fascinating person, with his lithe supple figure and charming black eyes, who speaks very good English.'

The Maharaja, although small for his years, was in fact thirteen. Soon after his father's death in April 1911 he had been crowned in Jodhpur and then taken to Wellington College in England by his great-uncle and regent Sir Pratap Singh (known by his many English friends as 'Sir P', after being knighted by Queen Victoria). Thakur Dhokal Singh, a friend of Sir P, had been appointed by him as one of the little Maharaja's guardians. The Viceroy had allowed the boy to attend the Coronation Durbar on the strict condition that he returned to school immediately afterwards.

After four hours of coaling, the ship steamed silently out of the harbour. The routine of life at sea was circulated to the passengers – breakfast at 8.30, luncheon at 1.00, dinner at 7.30. Prayers would be read daily, except on Saturdays. On Sunday morning a Divine Service would be held on deck by the Captain. Music, games and special entertainments were to be announced as the voyage progressed. The band was scheduled for most nights, but not the first, when Lord Bute's piper played the pipes on the second class deck after dinner, and all the maids and valets danced Scottish reels.

Like many Edwardian ladies, Lilah was an accomplished watercolourist and the sea skies constantly exercised her powers of imagination: 'A too lovely sunset – a wonderful pink and yellow glow, succeeded by soft greys and palest mauve and orange streaks in a velvety sky – after dinner it all looked like black velvet, sky and sea mingled together with wonderful stars overhead in the blackness – and mysterious flashes of light in the water which we were told was phosphorus.'

Within two days a choppy sea had blown up:

> We didn't think we could be bothered to dress for dinner, so we persuaded the deck steward to let us have some food up on deck, which was much nicer than having to sit for ages through a long dinner in the hot dining room... We talked to Alice Shaw-Stewart and the Spender Clays... And afterwards there was a dance – a queer night to choose for this entertainment, as the ship was rolling and pitching like anything. Colonel Mitford made me try and then I had to go on. It really was fun and one got used to the deck being at this [she does a drawing] angle most of the time. Lord Bute's piper played for the Scotch people to dance reels. They all took part, lurching comically, slipping and sliding against the rails...

Jean de Madre had taken to hovering. The Comte, whose father who had been the family lawyer to King Louis Philippe ('Roi des Français' in those troubled post-Napoleonic years when France oscillated between monarchy and republicanism), was an Anglophile and a horse lover. He had moved to England for the hunting and even more for the polo, which also took him to India. In England he was popular, and the unconscious butt of much gentle mockery. His polo team, the famous 'Tigers', had recently played against the All Ireland Polo Club in Dublin. Had Lilah by any chance seen the match? Somewhat implausibly for an Irish county lady who moved in viceregal circles, Lilah affected a complete lack of interest. Switching tack to the aesthetic aspect of the game, 'Johnny', as the Comte liked to be called, mentioned that he owned thirty polo ponies, enabling him to mount his team in a 'pretty colour scheme, with greys in the first chukka, bays in the second, chestnuts in the third, and so forth.'

The implication of great wealth was not lost on Lilah, who was beginning to find his attentions irksome. He asked her to dance but 'I got out of that,' she wrote. 'I thought it would be a bit too much! The old fellow will be a real bore before we are done with him. There is rather a fascinating ship's doctor aboard, but unluckily none of the ship's company is allowed to dance with the passengers, which seems an absurd rule – they all looked longingly on at the rest of us dancing.'

The weather deteriorated further. As the gale grew, Lilah's confidence in the *Maloja* waned. Driven against the long rollers of the Mediterranean, the ship pitched heavily. At every plunge she took in the seas over her bows, the flying spray drenching her decks from bow to stern. Considering that many of those on board were experienced travellers, the number of people prostrated was astonishing. Officers and passengers suffered alike, but the men worst of all because their quarters were forward, where the motion of the ship was felt most severely. After forty-eight hours, however as they neared Port Said, at the northern end of the Suez Canal, the gale lessened and at last the sea calmed down.

One after another the passengers began to reappear. When Lilah finally tottered to lunch she heard that hardly any of her friends had attended meals for at least two days. Relaxed again at at last, Thakur Dhokal told her of the loss of Sir P's luggage in a storm during its transportation from India to Britain in 1887. Divers recovered his jewels in time for Queen Victoria's Golden Jubilee but the disappearance of his clothes led to a fashion innovation, when Lady Rosebery persuaded a

Savile Row tailor to reproduce his idiosyncratic baggy trousers. Much photographed at the royal ceremonies and nicknamed 'jodhpurs' by the cartoonist 'Spy' in *Vanity Fair*, the trousers were immediately iconic and have since become a permanent fixture in the hunting and polo communities.

As they neared the port, with dusk falling, the Orient introduced itself: 'all turned into a soft grey and violet mist which hangs like a veil over everything, the very air seemed to change, sights and smells altered as if by magic; the sun dropped suddenly, the true Eastern sky which I had so often read of and seen in pictures, pale orange fading to dusky blue grey, made its appearance – it was as if in one afternoon we had been borne over hemispheres into an utterly different world.'

The ship dropped anchor opposite the Custom House and the town gradually lit up to glorious effect, heightened by the reflections of the lamps in the water. On dry land Lilah felt as unsteady as on the ship itself: the streets seemed to rock and sway in a most alarming manner. She and Sylvia used their ingenuity to dodge the Comte as he tried to accompany them on their walk 'amid the lighted cafés and the singing and shouting of the queer Eastern street vendors who poked their wares under one's very nose. We had to pinch ourselves hard before we realised it was a reality.'

They bought parasols and fans and returned aboard to watch the ship's coaling – a process which went on all night. 'The little black arabs, lithe and agile as monkeys, and jabbering freely all the while, carried the piled up baskets of coal from barges onto our ship – they looked like a swarm of ants, set in a grey green and soft black scheme of colours. But the dust and dirt from the beautiful operation was somewhat trying, and we soon went off to our cabins, much as I should have liked to watch them finish. So ended my first day in the East.'

4

Steaming East

Early next morning, as the ship left Port Said for the sixteen-hour journey down the Suez Canal, Lilah woke to see on the left of the narrow strip of water along which they were slowly making their way miles and miles of desert; on the right, banks studded with palm and fir trees. The calm water and baking sun elated her after four days of cold and rain in a Mediterranean storm. They passed barge after barge crowded with Arabs. On the shore edge, very close to the ship, were camels with riders in bright garments. One maintained exactly the speed of the ship, keeping its station off the starboard quarter for a good six miles. At intervals Bedouin with muskets appeared in robes of black and white, or men of the Egyptian Camel Corps in khaki coat, tarboosh and putties, mauve-grey breeches, brown bandoliers and brown goat-skin saddles. Lilah wrote in her diary that this would always be 'a golden day in her memory'.

A pilot came alongside the moving ship with the post and took letters for home. Lilah was passed a marconigram from her sister Olive, who had left London twelve days earlier on the *Goorka*, a smaller ship travelling to East Africa. Arthur Brodrick had discovered that the *Goorka* was just in front and still in the Canal. But Lilah never saw her.

The sun became even hotter, but Edwardian fashion and ritual continued to prevail as if in a London drawing room or at a weekend in a country estate. Suddenly everyone appeared in white – the men in duck suits and sun helmets, the women in cool white linens and thin muslin. Early shipboard encounters were fading into acquaintance or blossoming into friendships. Lilah was struck by the devotion to each other of the Butes, who sat at the next table to hers at meal times. John Bute, a paralytically shy polymath, was an energetic collector of paintings, furniture and *objets d'art*. He was also a devoted conserver of architecture, a commitment not confined to his own ten houses. He combined these cultural activities with an unfashionable preoccupation with business, where his interests were catholic and international, including plantations, mining and hotels. The Irishness of his gentle wife Augusta drew her and Lilah together, despite their very different temperaments.

An even more unlikely friendship formed with Alice Shaw-Stewart, who was close to the Souls – an exclusive society circle of people who prided themselves on their sensitivity and to whom the unpretentious Lilah had never felt attracted. Childless, tall and no beauty, Alice spent hours sketching and painting with Lilah or making their friends stand in groups to take a 'Kodak'. Lilah asked Thakur Dhokal, who wore dark green jodhpurs and an Indian jacket with a becoming crimson turban, to persuade the little Maharaja – who did not like covering his head in hot weather – to pose for a photograph in a turban.

Lilah had the gift of being able to concentrate on someone she was talking to as though he or she were the most interesting person in the world. Turning her searchlight on Thakur Dhokal she often sat with him to draw him out about India. The Comte de Madre, who was incontinently obsessive about lineage, lent her the *Golden Book of India*, a cross between *Burke's Peerage* and a biographical dictionary. This told her that 'thakur' meant feudal noble, a title just short of maharaja, but she quickly got lost in the book's account of the maze of historical and family connections between Dhokal's home state of Udaipur and the other great princely Rajput states of Jodhpur and Jaipur.

In his exquisitely idiosyncratic English Thakur Dhokal gently described the difficult childhood of his ward, Maharaja Sumer, the heir to the Jodhpur throne. On the premature death of Sumer's debauched father earlier in the year, the boy's great-uncle Sir P had resigned as ruler of the tiny state of Idar to assume his guardianship. It had not been easy. The India Office normally made a point of keeping control of the princely states through resident ministers during the minority of a maharaja. In this case, however, the Viceroy, Lord Hardinge, who shared the general respect for Sir P's character and did not want to offend the other semi-autonomous Rajput princes, had overruled the British Resident's objections and appointed Sir P as Regent.

It would be his second attempt at grooming a Jodhpur heir for the duties of state. An ascetic perfectionist, Sir P had thrown himself twenty

Lord Powerscourt, Lilah's father

The Hon. Lilah Wingfield

Powerscourt Castle, near Dublin, where Lilah was born and brought up

The coming of age at Powerscourt of Lilah's brother Mervyn. Lilah (centre) aged 13.

The Powerscourt ballroom

The Powerscourt estate workers formed a small corps

Powerscourt gardens – view from the house towards the Wicklow mountains

Lord Leicester, Lilah's grandfather, master of Holkham Hall

Lilah with her cousin on Holkham Beach 1902

Holkham Hall, where Lilah spent her childhood summer holidays

Coronation Durbar
of The King-Emperor
and Queen-Empress
Delhi, 12th December 1911.

Admit   The Hon'ble Lilah Wingfield

to Block   N   No. 51.

Uniform full dress.
Court dress for those not entitled to wear uniform.
Morning Dress permitted where Court dress not available.
Collar Day.

C. Henry McMahon
Master of the Ceremonies.

Invitation to the Durbar

On board the *Maloja* during the voyage to Bombay, (from left) Joan Campbell, Sylvia Brooke, Lilah's two chaperones Judy Smith and Arthur Brodrick; Captain Spender Clay, Sybil Fellowes, Mrs Spender Clay, and Alice Shaw-Stewart

Le Comte de Madre whose persistent courtship caused Lilah distress

The Maharaja of Jodhpur (centre), Thakur Dhokal, his guardian, and Sylvia Brooke

Coaling at Port Said

Sultan Ahmed Fadthel of Lahej, with his pipe and narcissi, en route to the Durbar

Lilah disembarks briefly from the *Maloja* in Aden

The *Maloja* (centre) docks at Aden. Bunting in preparation for the King's visit.

Lilah's first sight of Bombay Harbour November 1911

Bombay waterfront

years earlier into bringing up Sumer's father, in an effort to instil horsemanship and military prowess. Daily training, personally overseen by
Sir P, had begun with a morning run carrying a saddle, followed by an
hour riding bareback. During the last half hour the boy would be blind-
folded, with his arms tied behind his back and fireworks exploding to
freshen up his horse. Weak-willed, or broken by Sir P's boot camp
regime, Sumer's father had rebelled on coming of age, dismissed his
Regent and besmirched the family name by drunken and licentious
behaviour. He was stripped of his functions, exiled to a distant hill
station in Uttar Pradesh and placed in the Imperial Cadet Corps established by Lord Curzon 'to promote imperial understanding'.
Supposedly rehabilitated, he was reinvested with powers in 1905, but
disintegrated under the eyes of his son, Sumer, and died aged thirty-one
at the beginning of 1911.

Hearing this sorry story, Lilah looked with fresh eyes at the boy,
wondering sympathetically what chance he had of rising to the
challenge of high office. If he failed, it would certainly not be for want
of trying by his elders and betters. Determined that he should not go
the way of his father, Sir P had chosen Thakur Dokhal to help bring up
Sumer and make a man of him. It was a big responsibility. When the
young maharaja grew up, there would be 3,000 cavalry under his
command and as many infantry, together with a rich merchant state
covering 37,000 square miles of territory – the size of Belgium and
Holland combined.

Lilah jolted herself back reluctantly into the *Maloja*'s way of life. The
heat had now robbed dancing of all pleasure. For the next two evenings
she simply lay on a chaise longue drinking iced lemon. Sylvia made her
laugh with her caricatures of the more eccentric passengers, Lord
Cassalis, who looked like a pig, being the easiest. For a while they were
puzzled by two elderly spinsters who could be overheard offering a
running commentary on the other passengers. Then the penny dropped.
They were reporters for *The Lady's Pictorial*, one of whom was in daily
touch by marconigram with a contact on the *Medina*, enabling her to
regale her readers with vivid accounts of 'Charlotte Cameron's personal
experiences' on board the royal ship.

Stupefied by the heat, Lilah and Sylvia began to sleep on deck: they
were joined by the Duchess of Hamilton, Lady Cassalis and several

more. Lilah was worried she would end up with a stiff neck from a night outside, so she wrapped a shawl round her shoulders. The others were told they would get malaria: a vapour in the early morning off the shores of the Red Sea would bring the fever to anyone sleeping in the open. They paid no attention, happy just to have a cool night. They lay 'in rows on the deck on little white mattresses side by side ... it was heavenly lying in the wonderful starlit sky, hearing the swish of water against the side of the ship... At about 5 a.m. the grey misty dawn changed into the palest gold until the whole sky became one flaming rosy yellow glory.' The pleasure came to a sharp halt at six when their beds were taken away for the decks to be washed down.

With the ship now through the Gulf of Suez and out into the Red Sea, Lilah amused herself by entering the entire programme of competitions and obstacle races – all, that is, except for one contest, the passengers' favourite spectator sport, which was considered indelicate for ladies but the supreme challenge for male combatants. Two men sat astride a greased pole, which they were forbidden to touch with their hands, and struck at each other with pillows until one or the other fell off. Every class of passenger enrolled – marines, officers, the captain himself, servants, the barber, the fleet doctor, members of the band – but the prize always fell to the Royal Marines.

Sometimes she played quoits with the little maharaja, or entered the ladies' cricket match, undeterred by news from the upper deck that the gentlemen's cricket had been halted after a player had had his jaw fractured and four teeth knocked out by a wayward bat.

In the evenings there was music. Before dinner Lilah sang in the music room accompanied by Irene Denison on the mandolin, Sybil Fellowes on the violin and a male passenger on the piano. After dinner she sang a duet in the drawing room, prompting the Comte to a renewed effort at intimacy: 'Would she care to sing something for him alone?'

She would not. She tried to relieve her discomfort at the sense of being stalked by laughing about the Comte with her friends, but the effect was to make her feel guilty, as she recorded in her diary:

How very small-minded and gossipy one gets leading this sort of life, and having nothing to do but pick holes and criticise one's fellow passengers. Wasting time talking scandal about one thing or another! We all rag Colonel Mitford over his infatuation for a pretty little Miss Gauntlett. We composed a letter and had it given him by the deck steward, supposed to be from 'Mamma' Gauntlett, asking him his intentions! But he found out we had done it, so the joke fell flat... It is such a narrow circle and the world beyond this ship and its inhabitants seems so very far away.

Others, too, were paying court to Lilah, and she found them immeasurably more entertaining than the elderly Comte. 'He threatens to become a great bore to me. He is a regular gay dog of the worst type, which I did not discover at first, and is always on the look out to get me alone.' He would not let up. Next day she was 'obliged to talk to the Comte after dinner, as I was caught looking at the phosphorus in the water on the second class deck. I couldn't get away for a few minutes without being downright insulting. He is a wily old thing, he sees that I hate his odious love-making and paying compliments, so he tried talking to me in a really interesting way about France and the people and the revolution etc. I suppose he thinks he will get me to like him better so.'

Fresh light was now cast on de Madre's intentions:

This evening Judy told me that the Comte had told Lady Strafford earlier in the day that he had come on this voyage simply and solely for the purpose of finding a wife. He was very anxious to marry and considered there were more opportunities on board ship for getting to know a girl well than in any other place. He particularly wished for an English wife and did not want a very young girl – 'no inexperienced Miss of eighteen' – so he had set his sights on me. He enquired of my birth and position (I suppose he feared he might be making a misalliance!) and said he had determined to make my acquaintance as soon as possible on the voyage. I really cannot feel flattered at the offer for my hand from this horrid impudent old man, who must be 50 or 60 at least – and also I am not amazingly flattered that Lady Strafford should consider it possible that I might do worse than consider it, for she told Judy that he was a very rich man and would make an excellent husband. I would ten times rather marry the black boy who prepares my bath! Judy told her that I considered him an odious old man and that he was the one person on the ship I was always trying to avoid – I think Lady Strafford was quite disappointed. Now that I know his intentions, I shall be even more on my guard. But I don't think he can go on contemplating the idea now, as I have been downright rude to him whenever he comes near me; but it explains many things now that I have wondered about – like his loathsome way of looking me up and down when he passes me on the deck.

Within the day the story of Johnny's marital ambitions had gone round the ship. Lilah was 'unmercifully chaffed by everyone, especially Captain Spender Clay, who will keep asking when the wedding is'.

The next port offered Lilah the prospect of a brief respite from shipboard society. She had been warned about Aden, a strategic refuelling station for ships travelling to and from the East. In polite London society it was referred to in biblical language as the Abomination of Desolation (in military circles it had cruder names). Her very religious nanny had told her that the port was old as time itself, the birthplace of Cain and Abel. As they drew near she saw the sinister, cinder-coloured, purpling mountains, the relics of an ancient volcano, towering above the harbour. On land there was not a green leaf or blade of grass, only dry, greyish sand with sharp arid rocks. Armed against the sun in a topee, a green-lined sunshade and blue sunglasses, she left the ship with Sylvia at the first possible moment to make the most of the four hours before departure.

Despite the garrison port's barren appearance, Lilah found romance in the ancient lines of fortification, wall within wall. The foreshore was festooned with a spray of bright materials and bunting in preparation for the King's arrival in the *Medina* in four days' time. To visit some tombs five miles away, Sylvia and Lilah booked a strange-looking small covered carriage driven by a young black boy dressed only in a loin cloth. They shot off at a terrific speed, passing a large crowd along the main street, where the houses were built on one side only. Then they were immersed in swirls of colour, as they entered the market place where East met West: Sikhs, Pathans, Bengalis, Parsis, Somalis, Arabs, Negroes, Jews, Greeks and Levantines. Out of the small town, the road turned sharp and rocky; they passed 'camels with contemptuous faces and an air of mystery and little hut dwellings I found fascinating and delightful'.

Back on board, with only three days left before their arrival in India, Lilah felt life on the ship becoming ever more surreal, as if it must go on forever, this isolation on the sea with nothing beyond and nothing behind. All that people now talked about was what to wear at the end-of-voyage fancy dress dance. The Comte followed her round the deck seeking her advice – should it be the orange polo vest with its hand-embroidered Indian tiger on his chest, he wondered, or would his Quorn hunting pink be better, if it wasn't too hot for that?

Lilah's responses were increasingly monosyllabic: 'De Madre has grasped at last that I can't bear the sight of him, I think – he looks as sulky as a bear whenever he sees me.' Sylvia went as a Quaker girl, Judy as a geisha with a kimono and flowers in her hair. One man, to loud applause, went as a suffragette. Lady Hamilton went as Marie Antoinette, Sybil Fellowes as the Queen of Sheba, Lilah as an Irish colleen – the same costume, set off by the same plaited hair, that she had worn at the Savoy charity dinner before the voyage. Now she wore it again, exchanging the red Galway flannel petticoat for some crimson muslin she bought in the ship's barber's shop, which doubled up as a general store. Unable to stand the heat in the traditional Irish plaid shawl, she borrowed a multi-coloured silk kerchief from the purser to wear around her shoulders. The reporter from *The Lady's Pictorial* picked her out in her December column as 'very handsome'.

The last day on board turned into the roughest of the voyage. A fierce cyclone had developed soon after they left Aden. The Captain was worried that the royal ship would be in the thick of it. In spite of the foul weather, there were speeches of congratulation to the Captain at the final dinner on the success of the *Maloja's* maiden voyage. Lilah was given a photograph of the ship and collected autographs around it from her friends. Thakur Dhokal and his maharaja pressed her to make contact if she went to Jodhpur. De Madre, looking hard into her eyes, bade her farewell in the passageway: they would meet again in Delhi, of that he was sure. He would be with the Maharaja of Rutlam, a minor state. He would look in on her encampment in the 10th Hussars sector.

After twenty-four hours of rolling and pitching, on the morning of

28 November Lilah was woken by a sudden stillness. The *Maloja* had dropped anchor in Bombay. Weak from sea-sickness, she opened her porthole and leaned out. All around her were myriads of small boats and large steamers on a smooth oily sea – and beyond that, in the pale grey light of dawn, misty blue mountains and banks of gold-tipped clouds. She packed slowly, turned down Lord Iveagh's suggestion of an early morning visit to ancient cave temples on an island in the harbour, and at a gentle pace took a motor launch into the port. The special train to Delhi was leaving in the evening. She had half a day to drink in her first encounter with the East.

5
The Tented City

In the hubbub on the quay, with decorations for the King's arrival fluttering and flapping in the sea breeze, journalists crowded around. *The Times* reported: '...the arrival of the *Maloja* this morning has filled the chief meeting places of the city with a host of distinguished visitors. They complain of an unpleasant voyage ... but as they are mostly proceeding immediately to Delhi they will soon be consoled by an agreeable change of climate.'

Lilah and Sylvia were handed letters from Sylvia's brother Basil and from the Colonel of the 10th Hussars, Colonel Barnes, an old friend – in his imagination, an old flame – of Lilah, welcoming them and explaining what they were to do on arrival in Delhi if they could not be met. They were also greeted by two bearers and two ayahs, Rosie and Franzina, with rings in their ears and noses, bare feet and cotton saris. Arthur Brodrick dispatched the ayahs with twenty rupees each to buy themselves something warm to wear in Delhi and instructions to arrive at the train promptly by seven. Judy was independent – she had brought her own maid with her from England.

The cool of the early evening as they drove into the town in a hooded four-wheeled carriage refreshed them after the unseasonally intense heat of the day. They shopped for the journey ahead in narrow streets crammed with animals and a bustling crowd, their different senses assailed by a cacophony of clanging bells and music, spicy cooking smells, and intense, radiant colours. Lilah 'nearly screamed for joy' to Sylvia as they passed a water carrier with 'bare brown shapely limbs and turbaned head, his long leathern bottle dripping with water', like the pictures she had been allowed to look at on Sundays in her illustrated Child's Bible. Slowly the musky scented twilight subdued the bright patterns of the day and the setting sun threw mysterious shadows across the streets. 'Only fourteen days ago I was in smoky foggy London... It is unbelievable and impossible that

I have arrived in India at last – that my dream is realised. It all seems to have come so quickly and so easily.'

At seven o clock they reached the station, waved to one or two *Maloja* friends on the platform and found their ayahs already making up their beds, deftly smoothing out sheets and pillows and tucking in blankets. Lilah shared a three-berth compartment with Sylvia and Judy. Communication with Arthur would be intermittent, as there was no connecting corridor between the carriages or compartments. But the accommodation was more spacious and lighter than in English trains, the main inconvenience being that they had to carry soap, towels and a heavy basin to their little *en suite* bathroom. At meal times they would meet up with Arthur in the dining car when the train had come to a standstill, and then wait patiently until the next station to scurry back to their carriage.

For two clammy days and two sharp cold nights the train sped across a thousand miles. They adjusted to the changing temperature by raising or lowering the three layers of window in the hollow wall of the carriage – a shutter, a glass-paned inner window and a fine wire mesh between the two to let in the air and filter out some of the incoming engine soot, insects and dust. When the windows were closed an electric fan was on hand to relieve the oppressive closeness of the compartment.

Lunching in the train with the Mar and Kellies, who were on their way to stay in the Viceroy's camp, Lilah became so engrossed in the landscape that she could hardly bear to talk to them. Through the window she could see grey monkeys with white chests and very long tails darting in and out among the trees, parakeets, mynahs and crows, carts drawn by great horned bullocks, fields full of mimosa trees, palms and scrub, and peasants in the fields washing their clothes in muddy streams.

Small stations came at intervals of no more than half an hour. At each stop Arthur Brodrick diligently appeared at the compartment door with oranges, nougat and tangerines; sometimes Lilah stepped out onto the platform to be instantly surrounded by a swarm of small boys, natives in brilliant turbans and naked men protected only by loin cloths, all bargaining, begging, stealing or performing mesmeric feats of conjuring. Faced with the stunning novelty of this assault, Lilah confided to her diary that the whole framework and all the preconceptions of her English existence, with its formalities and rules, had abruptly become irrelevant. Life in India was outside the pale of those rigid conventions: it was unpredictable, bewildering – but it was life!

Half way through the journey colonial reality reasserted itself as Lilah's train halted for an hour in a siding to let the Viceregal Express overtake it. They arrived exhausted, to be met at Delhi station by Sylvia's 23-year-old brother Basil, a captain in Colonel Barnes's 10th Hussars. Sylvia flew into his arms. It had been four years since they had last been together.

They set off on the eight-mile journey to their quarters in a tonga, a two-wheeled horse-drawn covered cart assigned for their personal use for the two weeks of their visit. Travelling through Delhi – 'a small entirely native place, not a big cosmopolitan city like Bombay' – they continued north. Ahead of them the Tented City appeared and for the first time Lilah had a glimpse of the scale of the Durbar preparations.

The City had been assembled with unparalleled speed. Much of the site was on the ground of the 1877 and 1903 Durbars but it was only in July that the survey had been completed and the twenty-five square miles staked out for the encampments to occupy. The rough swamp marshland, which in summer had been parched and barren desert, had been levelled and seeded to create a smooth grassed plain. Despite crippling strikes in England and the shipwreck of several loads of equipment en route, the work had been finished on time. The narrow gauge railway, with its six-platformed terminal and its eighteen little satellite stations, had opened as recently as 10 November. Along this, engines borrowed from military reserves ferried the encampments' passengers on tracks laid by Sappers. By the time the Hussars arrived on 25 November, water pipes and electric light lines, farms, grain stores, a hospital, a post office and numerous shops were in place. Nine miles of metalled roads and thirty miles of tracks (oiled on the King's route to keep down the dust) had been laid on foundation stones carried to the site on their heads by native women.

The pitching of the thousands of tents had been delayed by a deluge of rain. Having seen the already erected ones reduced to sagging shadows of themselves (until the sun had miraculously revived them), Sir John Hewett, as chairman of the organising committee, decided to leave the completion of his virgin city to the last possible minute. The final peg had been hammered in shortly before Lilah's arrival. The term

'City' was no exaggeration of Sir John's achievement – no less than a quarter of a million people would be housed under canvas and provided with all the necessities, as well as most of the luxuries of modern life in the largest and most sophisticated encampment ever assembled.

The tonga came to a halt on the far outskirts of the City at Camp 277, where the illustrious 10th Royal Hussars (the Prince of Wales's Own) were stationed. They were greeted by Lilah's former admirer Colonel Barnes who apologised profusely for not being at the railway station to meet them – he had been on parade. 'It is some time since I last saw him, not since he was made Colonel of the 10th – he seemed to have grown older and quieter, I suppose from added responsibility.' Colonel Barnes's promotion was a reflection of an already distinguished military career which would become even more distinguished in the First World War. He had fought in two of the Boer War's most deadly actions, become a friend of the daring young Winston Churchill in South Africa, and had been wounded, decorated and seen service on the General Staff – all before reaching the age of forty.

They unpacked and took their bearings. For years Lilah had nursed a romantic vision of Indian tent life, derived from the letters of Lady Mary Hobhouse, an English visitor to Lord Curzon's Durbar in 1903. For the next sixteen days this unaccustomed shelter, so long a creature of her imagination, would be her home. Her initial impression confirmed her optimism. The size and elegance of her tent would allow her to entertain visitors for tea, conversation and music. A large bed stood in an alcove at the back. A wardrobe and a chest of drawers were in a separate dressing room thrown out behind. The two ayahs washed and pressed Sylvia's and her clothes, cleaned their tents and brought in a thick tin tub for washing and bathing. The ayahs themselves had a small tent outside and were always within call. But there was no getting away from the dust; it was everywhere and no sooner had a surface been wiped than it returned to cover it again. The water carriers sprinkled the roads from their goatskin *masaks* from dawn to dusk but though their efforts settled the dust for a while, the sun soon dried it out and the lightest breeze set it blowing again.

The first night started well enough, with Basil taking Lilah and his sister to the Mess tent, where from now on they would meet for meals.

Inside a large marquee a plain reception room led to a drawing room, with side rooms for cards and smoking, then through a long passage to the dining room and the kitchen beyond. The atmosphere reflected the simple efficiency of the soldiers' way of life. At eleven o'clock, after an entertaining dinner sitting next to Colonel Barnes, Lilah walked back happily to her tent, where she found her ayah on the floor snoring heavily, as if intending to spend the night there. She woke to explain that she was just guarding the tent until the return of her mistress. Lilah told her she needed no help with undressing, but she was happy to have the cloying dust brushed out of her thick, waist-length hair.

That night she could neither sleep nor get warm. The intense stillness contrasted with her weeks of confinement in a rolling ship's cabin and a rattling train compartment. Some time after three she was alarmed by the sinister almost human howl of distant jackals. Colonel Barnes had mentioned that these wolf-like animals had been known to enter tents at night, and Basil had tactlessly added that they sometimes bit people ('lots of the boys often went out jackal sticking, a great sport'). As dawn broke, an odd scuffling sound turned out only to be crows slithering down the canvas roof. Sylvia pulled her bed into Lilah's tent, to calm them both. At least it was unlikely to be rats – the Viceroy had had 90,000 rats put down before the camp opened.

Next morning Lilah recovered, lying in bed luxuriating in the sense of space and slowly letting the sun steal in to warm her through. She looked appreciatively at her chintz-covered armchairs, the bookcase and lavish Kashmir rugs spread over the brick floor, the desk with its electric lamp, pen-and-ink-holder and blotting paper – all the familiar furniture of a civilised room.

Less exhausted by the night, Sylvia left to go riding with Basil, who looked in to say that he had been released by Colonel Barnes from military rehearsal to escort them wherever they wanted to go. 'Basil and I call each other by our Christian names – he treats me with no formality, just like a sister – he comes in without any ceremony and talks and smokes, sitting on our beds.'

Their first event was the 17th Lancers' polo match. All the *beau monde* was there, transposing onto Indian soil the familiar social mores of England. The Comte de Madre was in his element, preening himself among the players and spectators, but too occupied, Lilah hoped, to have seen her. Between chukkas she ran into Arthur Brodrick, who was staying in an India Office camp, and felt a twinge of guilt that she was neglecting him. But she did not feel she had the right to ask him up to the Hussars for a meal. Basil introduced her to the officers' wives, Lady Helen Mitford and Mrs Ruby Gibbs, and she re-met some *Maloja* acquaintances and old friends from England, several of whom were staying with maharajas in the Tented City and bubbling with descriptions of the luxury and magnificence of their camps.

Throughout the previous week ten or twelve maharajas a day had been arriving on special trains with 66-foot carriages lined with mirrors and upholstered in silk and plush leather (and in one case a worship room of white marble). Each had been met by his resident, or political officer, with a guard of honour and a band. As the Ruler walked along the red carpet to his magnificent waiting carriage, a gun salute was fired, and his state's flag was raised as the band struck up a stirring welcome. Meanwhile coaches with covered windows discreetly conveyed the ladies in purdah to the encampment. Many of the maharajas were themselves polo players and could be seen mingling with their English guests at the match.

Lilah sat with Colonel Barnes, who had evidently made a point of going to the match to be with her. As the days progressed he figured frequently in Lilah's diary. He sought her out, sat beside her at meals, educated her in the intricacies of life in the Tented City and played cards with her after dinner. He would, however, have been disappointed if he had read what she wrote about him. There is admiration for him as a leader of men, but as before when he courted her in England, there is no hint of anything more than friendship on her part. On 1 December she notes that he has to dine with the Commander-in-Chief, so cannot go with her to the dance given by the Chief Commissioner of the Northern Provinces, the formidable soldier scholar Sir George Roos-Keppel. Another day she notes that he must rise at six for a regimental rehearsal. But these jottings reveal only curiosity towards the life of a senior officer in the Hussars.

Colonel Barnes was undoubtedly the man to turn to if there was a problem. One matter was particularly pressing. The King would shortly be reaching Bombay. He was not an accomplished rider and for his State Entry into Delhi his equerry had rejected both Sir P's high-spirited horse and the Viceroy's charger, a coal black thoroughbred of seventeen hands. At short notice Colonel Barnes had been instructed to find a quieter animal, but it was proving frustratingly difficult.

Meanwhile Lilah had been exploring, doing the round of the bazaars in Delhi and walking the length of the Chandni Chowk, reputedly once the world's richest street, where she bought two jade necklaces, one pink and one green, and ended up at Mr Schwaiger's celebrated carpet shop at the Kashmir Gate. Afterwards she climbed the Ridge which commanded the north-east approach to the city. This ridge was famous, Colonel Barnes told her, 'for being held against the enemy longer than any other spot in Delhi during the Mutiny'. She walked along the mound and gazed down on the tents, seen from this height as a jumble of different sizes and shapes stretching away in an ocean of white dots across the plain. As she descended, the chaos of her earlier impression resolved itself into a carefully designed canvas town, intersected by broad smooth roads with familiar signposts such as 'The Mall', 'Princes Road' and 'King's Way', where all the principalities and powers of India were assembled in a single place – the Viceroy and his council, lieutenant-governors and chief commissioners, Hindu and Muslim princes and ruling chiefs, men from the plains, men from across the border, from Bombay to Calcutta from Peshawar to Madras, Sultans from Arabia and the regions near Aden – all with their own retinues and troops.

With only two days to go before the King's arrival, Colonel Barnes asked the Viceroy's ADC, Captain Bigge, to give Lilah a tour of the Royal Camp, which was set in eighty-five acres of green lawns and gardens entirely of roses from India. The Viceroy's wife had commissioned simple furniture and embroidered materials from Indian craftsmen. The Queen's suite was lined in *vieux rose* silk, the King's in Star of India deep blue. In every room were open fires as well as electric radiators. Lilah, however, was not impressed: she thought the royal quarters 'like a governor's camp on tour, neat but not gaudy, comfortable but not the luxury I expected... I have heard so much about the opulence of the Maharajas' tents. That is what I really want to see.'

She was revelling in every minute of freedom from the controlling influence of her mother. An invitation from the Mitfords for an excursion drew a characteristic diary entry.

Helen sat in front with her husband, who drove the team of four horses. On the second seat, Colonel Barnes and Basil sat, with me in the middle. I *loved* the drive. We went up into the country away from Delhi, drove along the old trunk road that runs all the way from Calcutta to Peshawar – with low carts drawn by camels, the wide and desolate country stretching away in the distance, jackals crossing our path and running away to ground amongst the bushes. We came back in the dark, with the lights of all the camps shining through the gloom, a smouldering red glow in the distance.

Arriving back at the Hussars' Mess, they heard that two Punjab staff camps had caught fire – a regular hazard in the Tented City. The men in the lookout towers had not whistled the alarm in time to prevent four of the tents burning to the ground. Indians were, by all accounts, highly superstitious. In Bombay earlier in the day the flag that was hoisted on the King's arrival had stuck at half mast, resisting every effort to raise it further. This too was considered a bad omen. Lilah herself had a touch of Irish superstitiousness. Yet something told her that the Durbar would live up to her expectations.

6

The Maharajas' Tents

Lilah's social life soon became hectic – '… large coroneted and gold lettered invitations come in for us at all hours…' State functions mingled with private dances, including one to be given by the Maharaja of Indore with Lady Bute who was staying with him. The idea came to Lilah to deliver her acceptance card personally, taking the opportunity to visit some of the Maharajas' establishments on the way to the Indore camp and back.

After breakfast she set off with Arthur Brodrick in the tonga, going south past the amphitheatre to Coronation Road, the starting point for where most of the leading ruling chiefs' camps were situated. Arthur had consulted his Indian Civil Service friends, and had formed a plan of those grandees most worth visiting, whether for historical interest or for the sheer glamour of their tents.

Of the nearly 600 princely states not all were represented in Delhi. Some of the tiny principalities were mere dependencies of larger states; some princes could not afford to travel long distances with retinues of soldiers, servants, carriages, horses, camels and elephants. (One who did come had to be forbidden to bring his two tigers.) It was hard to keep count, but in the end about 475 chiefs settled in for the Durbar.

As the tonga turned into Coronation Road, with its triumphal arches and its riot of colour and sound, Lilah sat amazed at the waving banners, the bunting, the glare and glitter of coloured electric lights, the noisy confusion of twenty languages, ox-wagons, rickshaws, buffalo carts, hooting chauffeurs in Cadillacs, bell-laden camel-carts, bicycles, silver palanquins and carriages with horses fresh from the country that had never seen a crowd before. To the left and right of the road each archway led to a semicircular drive and a large garden encircled by convolvulus hedges in flower. Otherwise, no two camps were the same – the chiefs had gone to inordinate lengths to compete with each other in honour of the King Emperor. Geography combined with precedence to dictate each camp's position. The signs seemed endless – Malerkotia, Pataudi, Jubbal, Chamba, Bilaspur, Chatarpur, on and on, places of which Lilah knew nothing but the mysterious aura of the names.

First on Arthur's list was the Sikkim and Bhutan encampment, from the East Himalayas bordering Nepal and Tibet. A series of flying canopies led to a reception tent appliquéd with a spectacular embroidered phoenix and a Garuda, king of birds, symbols of triumphant aspiration beyond all human hope. Inside was a display of ancient Chinese tapestries, scrolls of events in the life of Buddha and a carved painted altar on a silk canopy. There was magic in the seven precious golden emblems of the Emperor of the World and his Queen, 'whose touch is happiness', with her gem beside her that could fulfil every wish and the wheel with a thousand spokes that could take the rider wherever he desired.

With a crowd of sightseers ahead, they abandoned the tonga and walked on to the Jammu and Kashmir archway, a pair of gigantic 36-foot-high dark black walnut wood gateposts attached on either side to fretted screen panels. Threading their way through the crush, they were courteously received by the Maharaja's private secretary, who interpreted for them the carvings of the fruits, ferns and plants of the kingdom. The 236-foot-long ensemble was a copy of Kashmir's ancient Pandretton Temple, commissioned to illustrate the skill of Kashmir's craftsmen. It had been five months in the making and at the end of the Durbar would be presented to the King Emperor. The secretary led them on past splashing fountains to tents lavished with all the luxuries of Central Asia.

Known as the Land of the Happy Valley for its spiritual and natural beauty, Kashmir, in the far north of India bounded by the high Karakorams and the West Himalayas, was home to a unique diversity of religions – Buddhist, Hindu, Sikh and in the most populated area Muslim. The elderly Maharaja, an orthodox Hindu who prayed twice a day, rated a 21-gun salute, the maximum allowed to a ruling chief, and maintained the largest body of troops of any of the states, which he regularly offered to the British Army. Even when his predecessor wavered during the Mutiny, Kashmir's native troops had been steadfast. The Maharaja would be taking a leading role in the Durbar and was on the list to receive an honour from the King.

On the opposite side of the road from Kashmir was the camp of the Nawab Begum of Bhopal, India's seventh leading state with a 19-gun salute, famous for being the only kingdom ruled by a female chief. With its rather ordinary entrance, it was not on Arthur's list of places to visit. Lilah, however, was longing to meet its far from ordinary occupant. She peered through the archway at the yellow curtains behind which Her Highness lived in Muslim seclusion, but having no introduction she moved reluctantly on. Her post-Durbar travel plans included a journey to Bhopal and she was determined to get to know the remarkable woman who presided over a million Muslim inhabitants.

After registering her acceptance for Lady Bute's dance, Lilah walked to the exuberantly luxurious camp of the Maharaja of Patiala, who had succeeded to the throne at nine but had recently reached the age of twenty-one and been vested with full powers by the Viceroy. As the premier Sikh of the Punjab, Patiala was one of a number of rulers, including Jaipur and Jodhpur, who were entitled to a 17-gun salute. In the Mutiny, his father and his grandfather had both shown exceptional loyalty, which the British had rewarded with honours and territory.

A fine cricketer and polo player, who had just returned from captaining the All-India cricket team in England, the young Maharaja was regarded as promising material for high office as ruler of a near-autonomous state. He was, however, reputed to have a voracious sexual appetite and had inherited his father's extravagance, owning India's first private plane and inhabiting a sprawling grandiose palace surrounded by statuary and artificial hills, with a racecourse and polo ground, both immaculately manicured. Lord Curzon's dismissal of the family as 'frivolous spendthrifts and idlers' and of his father as 'little better than a jockey' should have sounded a warning, but the India Office ignored it, as they did the well-known fact that he had already kept a harem of 350 women.

Lilah walked through the Patiala gateway of white and gold lions surmounted by a gold cannon to a glorious open *shamiana* – a ritual pergola – lined in silk and satin and with two gold thrones. Beside it stood a small tent for reading the Sikh holy book, the Granth. The *shamianas* were of crucial symbolic importance to the Durbar. Each senior Maharaja had one in the centre of his encampment, where he would formally receive the official visit of the Viceroy. The Patiala camp, including its *shamiana*, was considered the ultimate in appropriate high taste by the bureaucrats of the India Office.

At the junction of The Mall they were met at the Nizam of Hyderabad's encampment by an aide who showed them tiger skins and portraits of the King and Queen hanging prominently in the tent. The most trusted of all the Maharajas and one of the select 21-gun fraternity, the fabulously rich Muslim Nizams, once satraps of the Empire, had steered clear of the Mutiny and been accorded the title of 'Faithful Ally'. Their 83,000 square miles of territory in Peninsular India, with its own currency and a population of ten million, was so important to the Raj that, on the recent death of the Nizam's father, Lord Hardinge had hastened to Hyderabad from the Viceroy's palace in Calcutta to acknowledge the heir in person: '... a long and hot train journey of three nights and days... It was worth it ... we became on very close terms... [From then on] he never took any step without first asking my advice.' Certainly there were grounds for optimism that the new Nizam would be an improvement on his father, who had died of alcohol poisoning and was addicted, according to another of Lord Curzon's acid observations, to 'the sloth of the seraglio'.

Skirting the Tented City's train terminal, Lilah and Arthur walked on to the Baroda enclosure. The interior walls of the reception tent were lined with delicate grey and pink silk and the furniture had been commissioned from carpenters and wood enamelers in Dabhoi and Sankheda to give employment to the state's craftsmen and to showcase their talent. The ambience was one of discreet quality. But there was more – much more – to Baroda than met the eye.

Each chief and his family had behind them at least a century's history of loyalty, ambivalence or disaffection towards Britain. As the Empire disintegrated, giving way to the East India Company and later to the Raj, many of the Maharajas had sought the Crown's protection from marauding Afghans or from each other. By 1911 every ruler depended on the Raj for his powers, his legitimacy and the education of his heirs. Within the subtle gradations of devolved authority, the Gaekwar of Baroda, perhaps the most formidable and controversial of the rulers, posed searching questions of Britain's governing capabilities. His powerful state of five separate territories between Bombay and Rajasthan, originally a satrapy of the Mahratta Empire, had had a chequered past. In 1870 the then Gaekwar, having poisoned his British Adviser with arsenic, had been deported to Madras and replaced by the incorruptible Sir T. Madhav Rao, an exceptionally gifted regent to the orphan territory who successfully grafted radical reforms onto its conservative traditions.

For all Rao's brilliance a family successor had to be chosen and adopted as the heir. By custom this required superiority not of birth but of character. The next Gaekwar, a distant relative, was discovered in a local village by the powerful third wife of his deposed predecessor. Twelve years old and illiterate, he learned four languages, was given an education in the sciences, philosophy and history and was trained in politics and administration. So precocious was his ability that in 1881 at the age of eighteen he was given ruling powers over two million Barodans. Now thirty-eight, his had been a meteoric rise from obscure peasant to the position of His Highness Sayajirao Gaekwad III Sena Khas Khel Shamsher Bahadur Farzand-i-Khas-Inglisha Maharaja of Baroda, the illustrious owner of the tent where Lilah now stood.

The Gaekwar was at first regarded by the Raj as an exemplary prince. The honeymoon, however, did not last long. He was an effective reformer when in residence, but he travelled abroad too much and he was not sufficiently subservient. Worse, he permitted Barodan newspapers to print articles critical of the Raj and was known to meet seditious intellectuals at 'unrecognised' institutions. The India Office began to keep a file on him. In 1903 he had boycotted Lord Curzon's Durbar. Yet it was hard to present a convincing case for removing him, since his was one of the best run of all the princely states and his image was the diametric opposite of London's usual bugbear, the play-boy prince. To the great irritation of Government officials he had also been a favourite of Queen Victoria, who had given him a portrait of herself set in diamonds as well as the Grand Cross of the Star of India.

On his recent visit to London for the Coronation, the Gaekwar had planned to stay on in Europe 'to learn more about Western institutions', but in reality to avoid having to pay homage to the Crown at the Durbar. Lord Crewe, however, had summoned him to the Foreign Office for a frank conversation, after which he undertook to reach Delhi in time for the King's visit. Lord Hardinge's political department, highly suspicious of him, was watching his every movement. Of this

Colonel Barnes was well aware, but his discretion held him back from mentioning it to Lilah, who had given him no opportunity for intimate private talk. No matter. Within a few days, the Gaekwar problem would become dramatically evident to the whole world.

Lilah's Jodhpur friends, Thakur Dokhal and the little Maharaja, were not at home, but she had now arrived at King's Way, where the profusion of public expressions of devotion to the Emperor showed this to be the heart of the loyalist sector. None was more ultra-loyalist than the Maharaja of Bikaner, 'the Lord of the Desert', master of the famed Camel Corps from Rajasthan, which had fought with distinction in numerous foreign campaigns and would gain further battle honours in the Arabian desert during the First World War. The Maharaja's aide proudly showed them his life-size portrait of the King Emperor, flanked by a Highlander and a Greenjacket.

Lilah would have liked to stay longer to inspect some of the Bikaner camels close up to see their soft doe eyes, with their two layers of eye-lashes and their thick eyebrows. How on earth could these slow, sway-ing creatures run in a camel race later in the week? But Arthur was impatient to hurry on, for their next visit was to the camp of the famous cricketer Ranjitsinhji, the Maharaja of Nawanagar, where Lilah's two friends from the *Maloja*, Sybil Fellowes and Irene Denison, were stay-ing, along with a contingent of British aristocrats. 'Ranji', as he was known, had been at Cambridge, and was universally regarded as a cricketing genius, the world's finest batsman and the first Indian hero of the English cloth cap spectator through his scoring feats for Sussex and England. In 1907 he had reluctantly retired in his prime to fight a long and complex battle for recognition as the legitimate heir of his home State of Nawanagar. He had cut an impossibly glamorous figure on his arrival in Delhi in a silver carriage accompanied by retainers bearing before them the shield of state painted with the insignia of Nawanagar's power, his sword and dagger flashing across his bejewelled costume.

Sybil boasted that Ranji's was the most magnificent of all the camps. She showed Lilah round, laughingly describing opulent dinners where the guests were showered with garlands and sprayed with perfume. Over tea in the boudoir next to Sybil's bedroom, they caught up with each other's reaction to India. Not yet used to the glitzy princely taste, Lilah wrote:

I have never seen anything like the strange mixture of cheap English furniture, family heirlooms and gaudy barbaric splendour. In Ranji's huge reception tent there was for instance a large gold throne on a raised dais, and all around solid silver chairs, and on the floor and walls the most costly hangings and stuffs rich with gold, while round the walls were cheap bits of would-be English art furniture, wholly out of place.

Unknown to his British admirers, Ranji's extravagance was much frowned upon in official circles. The failure of the summer monsoon in Nawanagar had forced him to request a large loan from the Government to alleviate his people's famine. The Gaekwar of Baroda had offered to help by lending him money backed by a Government guarantee, but the Bombay Governor had turned this down. After the Durbar, he was humiliated by the imposition of a Financial Adviser on his administration.

As she returned to her own tent, Lilah's head was spinning with her glimpse of the Maharajas' way of life and the kaleidoscopic contrasts of India. Although her Irishness gave her an instinctive sense of what it meant to have divided loyalties, she was acutely aware how little she knew about the various states' histories and the complex relationships of their rulers to the Raj. But her Indian odyssey had only just begun. She was determined to make up for lost time.

7
Final Preparations

Lilah had seen in the Durbar encampments a dazzling selection of cere-monial objects, gold maces, jewelled swords, oriental carpets, state robes, embroideries, painted fans, hangings and gems from every corner of India. She had also picked up her first glimmer of under-standing of colonial politics. Enthralled by the country, she plied her more knowledgeable friends with questions. Colonel Barnes was excep-tionally well informed, but no one could have been encyclopedic enough to satisfy her thirst for enlightenment.

The Colonel's fondness for Lilah was becoming evident to everyone except, apparently, to her. But her persistent curiosity made him irritable, the result as much of physical exhaustion as of his inability to make progress with her beyond history lessons and rather heavy badinage. His responsibilities during the build-up to the King's arrival were increasingly arduous – drilling men, commanding parades, and, most demanding of all, conducting the rehearsals for the Durbar events. These were not going well, and the Viceroy had let it be known in no uncertain terms that he was alarmed. It was some consolation that the Colonel had finally found a horse for the King, a small dark bay of docile temperament. He had to admit, however, that its looks were unimpressive, a further cause for Viceregal displeasure.

Having missed the rehearsal for the State Entry, Lilah made an effort for the Colonel's sake to go to the amphitheatre with Sylvia to watch the final rehearsal. They did not stay long. All they could see were a sham King and Queen dressed in cotton robes sitting on chairs acting as thrones. In any case, they would be enjoying the real thing in a week's time.

Lord Hardinge was in a filthier mood than ever, and was heard muttering under his breath that the dress rehearsal was a complete fiasco. Apart from the shambles of the troop manoeuvres, he had had to correct several Maharajas over their bowing and their walking backwards as they left the royal presence. He was resigned to the non-appearance of the old Maharaja of Udaipur, who was 'unwell', but the Gaekwar of Baroda's absence, without any apology, was most ominous. No doubt Lord Crewe had knocked sense into him at their meeting in London and there was no reason to suspect that he would expose the King to embarrassment on Durbar Day in front of 150,000 spectators. Scotland Yard's reports, however, had put the Viceroy on full alert. And not only about Baroda. The Mutiny of 1857 was history, but history that might repeat itself. There were renewed stirrings of revolutionary independence. Acts of terrorism, 'violent outrages', were not uncommon. It was particularly concerning that the trouble had spread to regions such as the Punjab, which had always been loyal to Britain. An unspoken part of the Durbar's aim was to reinforce the authority of the Raj by getting the princes to proclaim their homage publicly to the King Emperor in front of their own people.

The Indore ball on 6 December was the first invitation Lilah had received from an Indian. She had high expectations but on arrival it became clear that there was rather too strong a British contingent for her liking, no doubt largely invited by Lady Bute. For all Augusta Bute's charm the evening began with oppressive formality. Lilah found herself caught between Lord Mar and Kellie – wearing the Royal Company of Archers' court dress of green with gold embroidery, and cocked hat with green feathers – and the shy Lord Bute, both behaving in the stiff, distant manner adopted by aristocrats on such occasions. As her Irish spirit was about to rebel – or somehow startle the two men out of their stereotypes – Augusta introduced her to the Maharaja and two of his retinue, one an opium trader, the other a jeweller, both of them also money-lenders and pawnbrokers. The official record described them as 'bankers'. 'The Maharaja was in pale blue satin brocade, gold trousers and turban, wearing wonderful jewels – from his neck and across his chest to below his hips a chain of emeralds and pearls, diamonds and an immense white sapphire. He told me he was married at fifteen. He could not understand that the Maharaja of Mysore preferred to stay in Maiden's Hotel in Delhi, rather than his own tent.' The Maharaja's charm was as dazzling as his clothes. But Lilah was impervious to it: '...there was something uncomfortable to me about his suaveness of manner.'

The young Maharaja, who had now reached the age of twenty-one, had returned home from his European travels in October to a public ovation from his subjects. The tour of Europe had gone well. Civil servants wrote of him: 'Travel had broadened his views and mental horizons. ... many English noblemen sought and courted his friendship. He was received everywhere' – that included the Butes and the Hamiltons in Scotland – 'and left a most favourable impression ...' Judged to be the right material to rule his state, he had been installed in November with powers to oversee law and order and the allocation of revenue – albeit within the limits of the colonial system, whereby the British Resident could intervene if necessary. In exchange for loyalty and good governance, he would be given protection: all being well, a liberal scattering of titles would follow and perhaps even the ultimate reward: an increased gun salute.

Lilah moved away gracefully, catching up with acquaintances from the *Maloja*. Joined by Thakur Dhokal, and released from the Anglo-Saxon conventions she found so stifling, she danced and danced, free at last to immerse herself in an India she was only beginning to discover. When the Durbar week was over, Thakur Dhokal would show her 'his' India, Rajasthan.

The evening ended early and Lilah returned to the Hussars' camp with Sylvia and Basil in a tiny car meant for two, driven by Gerald Stewart, a regimental friend of Basil. Sylvia was pressed against the steering wheel, with Basil clinging to Lilah from his perch on the running board – 'all four of us bellowing at the top of our voices "The Wearing of the Green" and being thrown all over the place. I should have been terrified: instead I was overwhelmed by a sense of remove and exhilaration and complete oblivion of everything at home in England. We narrowly avoided running into a bullock cart which, turning sharply to the left out of our way, lumbered down the side of the steep ditch.'

Still in a state of elation, the four went to the Mess tent for a midnight supper of sausages, poached eggs and lager. Lilah finally made it to bed at 2.30 a.m., delighting in Gerald Stewart's company and laughing all the way to the tent entrance with him. Next day the Durbar proper would begin with the King's State Entry.

8

The State Entry

The State Entry of the Emperor King and his Empress Queen – the first of the two great events of Durbar week – was to start at a symbolic landmark, the Red Fort in South Delhi. Built in the seventeenth century by Shah Jehan, the most charismatic of its emperors, the Fort had been the Mughal capital until the last emperor, Bahadur Shah, was exiled in 1857 to Rangoon after the Indian Mutiny. The finest and most magnificent of all the Mughal fortress settlements, it was a complex of halls, palaces, pavilions, water courses and gardens, its marble rooms once decorated with gold and precious stones and lustrous polished mosaics. These had all been looted by the various conquerors of Delhi, the last being the British soldiers in 1857.

The 10th Hussars were up hours before dawn to line the streets and enforce the security curfew that the Viceroy had ordered in the city centre. It was icy cold in the pitch darkness, with a frosty mist coming through the tent door. Lilah reluctantly left her warm bed with its thick Jaeger blankets, shivered briefly in her bath, then joined Sylvia for breakfast at 7 a.m. They drove in a brake to catch the unheated little train. It was 'horribly slow', but they reached their reserved place in good time.

The King, in field marshal's uniform with a sun helmet hiding much of his face, arrived at 10 a.m. at Salemgarh, the nearest station to the Fort. As he alighted from the train a 101-gun salute boomed out from the ramparts, followed by a *feu de joie* (a rolling volley) reverberating two miles up to the Ridge and back again.

Waiting opposite the station under a pavilion to receive him were the Viceroy Lord Hardinge and a small selection of the grandest Maharajas. Two of these – the Maharaja of Bikaner and the Nizam of Hyderabad (in mourning for his father, and therefore dressed in black with a diamond aigrette on his turban) – were in exemplary standing with the Crown. The third, the elderly Maharana of Udaipur, bluest of blue blood, wearing a flowing white and gold satin gown, posed more of a conundrum to the Viceroy. He was happy to receive the King on his home soil, welcoming him as an honoured guest, but his ancestors' proud resistance to the Mughals and his fierce sense of his state's independence had won him unique veneration from his peers and made it almost impossible for him to pay homage to a foreigner, however friendly or powerful. On the other hand since, unlike the Gaekwar of Baroda, he could not be suspected of condoning subversion, his sensitivities would be appeased for the duration of the Durbar and he had been granted a specially prestigious position within the King's personal entourage.

Grateful for the shelter as the sun's heat grew more intense, Lilah waited for two hours under a canvas awning inside the Fort's pink sandstone walls. Exhausted by her previous night's antics, she fell asleep. But she was jerked awake abruptly when the Chief Herald in a tabard blazoned with the arms of the Sovereign entered, followed by twenty-four trumpeters and heralds in tabards of crimson and gold, mounted on white horses. A huge blast from their silver trumpets proclaimed their Majesties' approach.

The King and Queen slowly crossed the drawbridge into the Fort and took their seats on two golden thrones to receive the presentation of high officials and representatives of every arm of the fighting forces. The King then received four veterans of the Mutiny (three Indian and one British), who drew themselves up and saluted after the fashion of their youth, with the hand parallel to the horizon.

The King moved on to greet the rest of the native princes in a short welcome. This had been scheduled to take place in the historic Bahawalpur tent, the most magnificent *shamiana* in India, adorned with ancient appliqué and heraldic signs. Disaster, however, had intervened: the glorious canvas pavilion had burnt to the ground during the rehearsals, the victim of a carelessly discarded cigarette. A simple replacement was hurriedly erected just in time for the State Entry. The seven-year-old Nawab of Bahawalpur gallantly paid his respects to the King and was met by a burst of sympathetic applause. Although the loss of the original *shamiana* deprived the occasion of much of its glamour, a chief from the Shan State was so overcome that he unwound his gold embroidered sash and laid it down at the feet of the King.

Before the cortège left the Fort another royal salute was fired, answered by a salvo from the Ridge, the sixty-foot-high hill spine, site of the crucial turning-point of the Indian Mutiny half a century earlier. Battery after battery roared and thundered so that all Delhi could know that the King was coming into the crowded town and the imposing camp beyond the Ridge, to spend ten days living among his subjects in their ancient city, for generations the Mughal capital of India.

The choice of the processional route through the Delhi Gate was considered as symbolically important as the King's arrival at the Fort. He would continue along the Via Sacra towards the cathedral Mosque, the Jami Masjid, where each Friday the Emperors had passed in a golden palanquin, shielded by noble footmen from vulgar gaze.

The royal cavalcade of twenty-eight of the King's staff led the procession. To avoid all doubt as to which was the King, Lord Hardinge had ordered them to keep fifty yards ahead of His Majesty, while he, Lord Crewe, the Duke of Teck and the other officers would keep fifty yards behind him. But the punctilious care with which the King and Hardinge had planned the Durbar entry over the last eight months contained a flaw. They decided not to follow the example of Hardinge's predecessor, Lord Curzon, who at the Royal Durbar eight years earlier had played the Viceregal part to the hilt, conscious of the impression on the populace and the ruling Princes of extravagant pomp and splendour. Processing in full regalia on a caparisoned elephant under a golden howdah, Curzon's had been a show fit for the representative of the greatest sovereign on earth. But now, the first time a reigning British monarch had arrived in person on Indian soil, the Emperor of Emperors appeared as an insignificant, virtually invisible, figure, seated uneasily on a small bay horse surrounded by taller, more imposing and better mounted military men.

The crowd of eager faces peered in vain at the procession in the hope of catching sight of their Emperor. The trouble was compounded by the vividly conspicuous Queen, who followed immediately after him in a sparkling open landau drawn by four horses and adorned by a huge golden fan and crimson and gold umbrella held over her head by her Indian attendants. There was only one thought among the onlookers: 'Where on earth is our King Emperor?'

As the lonely figure of the King rode anonymously down the processional route into the mile-long Chandni Chauk, the crowds looked at the Queen in all her glory and came to the conclusion that she must have left His Imperial Majesty behind in England. For a people who believed in the importance of the sight and touch of their God-Emperor, his imagined absence was a catastrophe.

To Lilah and her neighbours, the King's dismal appearance was 'rather a pity', but at least they knew he was present. Brushing aside her disappointment, Lilah allowed herself to be carried away by the magnificence of the unfolding spectacle:

> ...a mass of colour, a wonderful, really wonderful sight... After the Queen's carriage came an escort composed of the 10th Hussars, the glittering spear points of Royal Horse Artillery greeting the rising sun, the Governor-General's bodyguard, the Imperial Cadet Corps in white, gold, and blue, and the bright points of waving, dancing pennons [streamers] of the 18th Indian Lancers in scarlet and gold, the English Lancers and Dragoons in all their varied brilliance of uniforms with sun glinting on swords and gold trappings, a dazzling scene of splendour.

But this paled against what was to come. After the last regiment of the King's cavalcade had passed through the Delhi Gate, there was a signal from the Marshal. In a frenzied rush coachmen, grooms, servants and footmen poured out in their thousands to help their Lords mount their horses and camels or usher them into their coaches. The Maharajas of Hyderabad, Baroda, Mysore and Kashmir led the way, followed by rulers from every province in India. Beside each chief sat the Resident – his white-helmeted, blue-clad English Political Adviser, sometimes friend, sometimes not, drawn from diplomatic or military circles, his power derived from the Raj, but with all the nuances that relations with the Viceroy and his Maharajas involved.

Lilah begged a lift to the Ridge and flew off in the Mar and Kellies' car. The contrast between the formality of the King's progress in front and the Maharajas' wild caravanserai behind was so acute as to be almost painful. Her astonished senses took in the princes' gold and silver carriages, running footmen shouting to clear the roads, birds' plumes quivering, bells crashing, squadrons of marching attendants in coats of mail, and fierce Arab horses from Radhanpur snorting and prancing.

Meanwhile the King, continuing his slow procession amongst massed bands spilling out triumphal music, reached the Chandni Chauk. To the Viceroy this street in the heart of Delhi, with its mixed population, was the most dangerous point of the journey. It had long been the scene of murder and reprisals. On one side of the street the procession would have to pass right under the windows of the houses. So anxious was the Viceroy that he gave orders to arrest the city's 300 most dangerous troublemakers the day before the King's arrival. But there were to be no martyrs. They were to be well treated, well fed and made comfortable, and released from prison as soon as the King left Delhi. The Viceroy brought in 4,000 police from the neighbouring provinces, positioned a police officer at every window and sealed off the roofs. The backs of the houses were guarded by Indian troops. Nobody was allowed in or out after 6 a.m. During the five hours before the procession was due to pass through, the police searched every house from cellar to attic. The result was that at eye level in the city's most important street the view of the Royal procession was totally blocked. No criticism of these precautions appeared in the press. The general consensus was that it was a wise step for a strong Government to have taken.

The King left the city and reached the summit of the Ridge, where a reception committee awaited him. Speeches were made, the Royal Standard raised. Another salvo of guns burst out and he resumed his journey back to the Imperial camp in the Tented City.

As the final gun shot signalled the King's departure from the Ridge, all constraints vanished. Until that moment only the King's symbols of authority had been permitted. Now Indian princes' ancient banners were unfurled and state flags raised up high – against a host of carved and painted emblems, centuries-old guns, bayonets, fans, screens and elaborate fly whisks. The Maharajas' procession had grown to five miles in length and swollen to 6,000 men strong. Under the azure sky and blazing hot afternoon sun, order gave way to riotous tumult, with pipes, joyful shouts, the beat of kettledrums, bards chanting, dancers whirling and acrobats wheeling in the dust to a strange music. The people from every part of India, even the reserved British, were swept up in an extravaganza of emotion.

To deafening cheers from the multitude, the cavalcade by-passed the

Ridge, taking their own route where there were no troops lining the way, and poured down Princes Road and King's Road to the Maharajas' camps. The *Times* correspondent wrote euphorically about the success of the King's State Entry, but he noted enigmatically that the wild exuberance of the native crowd was 'an unexpected reminder to the representatives of British India that there are elements in their immense country which take no heed of council halls, but must nonetheless be reckoned with'.

Enveloped by the mood, Lilah rushed back to the city to be even nearer to the action.

The jewels worn by the occupants of the coaches were a thing to dream of – great ropes of pearls and emeralds as large as pigeon eggs such as I have never seen before and so strange to see them adorning men... Then, too, came the camel Corps with two hundred Camels, a wonderful sight... The Begum of Bhopal, in pale blue burka circled with jewels, behind her carriage a grand banner given to her by Queen Victoria... her retainers in brown and white and gold sashes and brown turbans received an especially great ovation... She was so strictly veiled that only little slits allowed her to see out and not be seen. I want to meet her very much. Some of the native troops, especially the Sikhs, are magnificent men – with fine figures, and wonderfully noble cast of faces and good features, set off as they are by beautiful uniforms, which give a good-looking man such an imperial look. The Sikkim head-dresses were of gold and silver in the shape of mosques, minarets and pagodas with dangling things, and below large ear covers, and garments stiff with gold. The Chief sat in his carriage, his secretary on the box holding one of the huge mosque-like models on a cushion on his knees. Six retainers rode behind. The noise was deafening. Loud bells ringing on the carriages... The Gaekwar of Baroda was in pale blue silk and turban, and jewels that surpassed all before.

The Gaekwar was indeed there but there was no sign of the Maharana of Udaipur. The Viceroy's conciliatory approach towards this elderly, supernaturally revered figure had failed: after meeting the King at the Fort, he had quietly headed back to Udaipur.

Catching sight of the Maharaja of Jodhpur, with Thakur Dhokal behind him, Lilah waved, exchanged smiles and called out a greeting, inaudible above the clamour of the crowd. She felt a surge of pride at her friendship with this tiny exotic native prince, in his fine carriage with gold trappings, an embodiment of Jodhpur Maharajas past and to come.

There was more than mere decoration to the way the Rajas' bodies were swathed in jewellery from head to foot, leaving no skin visible. On board ship Thakur Dhokal had explained to her that a Durbar procession was a carefully crafted religious ritual, the core of all that kept the princely families compelling to their peoples. A ruler needed to be displayed to enhance his power; the public needed to see him to participate in that power. The objects he brought to a Durbar were as important as the clothes he wore, centuries-old decorative symbols which left interpretation to the viewer, allowing for differences in belief about religion and kingship. At the time Lilah had barely understood. But now his explanation illuminated the kaleidoscope before her eyes.

When it was all over, the Mar and Kellies dropped Lilah and Sylvia back at their tent. They arrived hungry and exhausted, lunched in the Mess and collapsed into bed for the rest of the afternoon. Basil returned much later, to wake them and mull over the day's proceedings. He confirmed that the troops lining the route had heard the grumble from the crowd that they could not see the King and the speculation that he had stayed in England, sending the Queen in his stead. But there was nothing anyone could do at that moment to stop the rumour spreading – as Basil said, they could hardly make an about turn and start lecturing the spectators.

In the regimental camps rival explanations for the King's low profile did the rounds. The most plausible version attributed it to caution on the part of the India Office, which was said to have banned an elephant ride out of fear that he would make an easier target for a nationalist bullet or that the gun salute would cause a repeat of the lethal elephant stampede in the Lytton Durbar of 1877. A more naïve version was that the King had himself deliberately chosen a horse to be less remote from the people. 'In that case he could at least have worn a special uniform, or driven with the Queen,' complained Sylvia, 'or have ridden a horse with a Royal Standard and a dozen standards around him.' Lilah loyally answered that it was typically modest of the King to wear a simple field marshal's uniform and ride unostentatiously with the men, showing himself as not only their chief but also their fellow soldier. Whatever the true explanation, they could all agree that the troops and the Maharajas had made the spectacle unforgettable. In Lilah's heart it was the Indian princes who had stolen the show.

The ancient Grand Trunk Road stretching from the North-West Frontier to Delhi and Calcutta

Bringing furniture into the Tented City

The Tented City, created for the Durbar fortnight, covered an area of twenty-five square miles

Lilah's ayah with Sylvia Brooke and Judy Smith

Colonel Barnes, commander of 10th
Hussars, off duty

Lilah with her ayah

Lilah on her grey mare – her first ride for many years

The Cadillac which took Lilah to the amphitheatre for the Durbar ceremony

The tonga lent to Lilah for the Durbar fortnight

A stray cigarette stubb sets alight the Punjab encampment in the Tented City

The Tented City at night: view from the hill above Delhi

Maharajas arriving in Delhi early December 1911

The Maharaja of Patiala: wearing the
famous Patiala pearls

Sir Patrap Singh, friend and loyal subject to
both Queen Victoria and King George V

The giant entrance gates to the Kashmir encampment

Triumphal arch with Maharaja's
encampments beyond

The Maharaja of Indore whom Lilah found
suspiciously suave

The people wait below the Red Fort before the arrival of their King Emperor

The garden party within the walls of the Red Fort

The King Emperor and Queen Empress on arrival in Delhi

9
A Walk with the Colonel

A perceptible sense of distance had started to develop between Lilah and the officers in the camp. She felt she was being assessed. Sylvia on the other hand had become one of the boys – riding each day, even going on jackal-sticking hunts with them. Not having sat on a horse for some years, Lilah had lost her nerve for riding. Nevertheless, in order not to be left out she forced herself to overcome her fear and accepted an offer of a horse 'so quiet that she could not possibly be frightened'.

Up first thing the next morning, clad in her riding habit and 'in mortal terror', she found the horse at her tent door. But to her embarrassment the animal keenly resisted all her efforts to get on him from a chair, 'jib-bing about all over the place'. At that point Helen Mitford's sister Kitty Vincent rode past on a calm-looking white mare and suggested swap-ping horses. Summoning up her courage, Lilah accepted the offer and trotted away alone towards the review ground. She looked back to see Kitty effortlessly mount and canter off towards the Ridge.

With relief Lilah felt her nerve return. She rode on down towards the King's camp. Her horse did not shy as it met Ranjitsinhji's rattling silver carriage and the camel-drawn carriage of some Punjab chief in the bustling commotion of Coronation Road, where Maharajas and their retinues were coming and going from the royal reception tent. The King had begun the three-day ceremony of receiving them. The Chiefs, each accompanied by seven nobles of high state office, had vied fiercely with each other in the magnificence of their entourages' appearance in the presence of their Emperor. The oriental scene before Lilah's eyes seemed to her like a court scene from an ancient Mughal miniature.

Those maharajas entitled to the privilege of meeting the King – seventy of them – would also receive a return visit from the Viceroy accompanied by the Secretary of State for India, Lord Crewe, an honour attended by all the pomp and ceremony befitting their princely rank. Lilah was curious to see how the Englishmen would adapt themselves to paying court to Indian nobility – a complete reversal of their normal role. She headed for the Patiala tent to watch Lord Hardinge walk towards the *shamiana* between lines of liveried servants, hand in hand with the Maharajah. Lord Crewe followed three steps behind them. Under the *shamiana*, the Viceroy sat stiffly side by side with the graceful, bejewelled Maharaja on elaborately embossed state chairs, surrounded by maces, fans of peacock feathers and the plumes of yak tails – a tableau of power elaborately crafted for display. Leave was formally sought and courteously granted to present the chief's court noblemen to the Viceroy, who was then symbolically offered a gold coin on a silk handkerchief – the sign of loyalty – which he touched and returned. After ten minutes the two walked slowly back, hand in hand again, to the awaiting carriage.

This ceremony – including the gold coin and the handkerchief – was enacted and re-enacted seventy times over three days, and was the product of the King's own imagination. Like his grandmother Queen Victoria, George V had a deep affection for India and an abiding sense that the Colonial administration treated its peoples with inadequate respect. He barred the use of the word 'native' in his presence and urged government ministers and officials to regard the Maharajas as equals who should be given a parallel role alongside the British in governing their states. To Lord Hardinge, who regarded the Indians as adolescents to be kept in order, and disciplined for offence or rewarded for good behaviour, this indiscriminate honouring of the Maharajas seemed a mistake. But his own reverence for the royal command left him no choice but to make the best of it.

That afternoon, chatting inconsequentially with Colonel Barnes about her rediscovery of the enjoyment of riding, Lilah noticed the awkwardness of a passing officer, Captain Annesley, who acknowledged his Colonel with patent embarrassment and hurried on. She wrote: 'Later that evening Basil told me that Captain Annesley had rushed into the Mess in great excitement to inform everyone he had seen the Colonel taking me for a walk. He was sure he was going to ask me to marry him then and there.' She tried to shrug this off as camp humour, but she suspected in her heart that she was fooling herself. That old difficulty of hers, her inability to be 'just friends' with men, had returned with a vengeance.

In the lead up to the Durbar on 12 December each day was filled with ceremonial and social engagements. As a peer's daughter Lilah had a ticket to the laying of the foundation stone of the statue of King Edward VII in a garden near the Red Fort. The Hussars would be prominent and Lilah wanted to go, but not alone. Helen Mitford, who planned to go riding, offered Lilah and Sylvia the Mitford buggy. Their seats in the Viceroy's stand were very near the King, whom Lilah was seeing for the first time at close range. He spoke with a strong clear voice, but she thought he looked rather unwell.

The next day was the start of the polo tournament, followed by a night tattoo with torchlit massed bands. On Sunday there was an outdoors state church service. They sat in the military stand and watched the King and Queen arrive behind a mass of bishops and clergy to sit alone on a raised dais throughout the service. 'There were miles and miles of troops in white helmets and scarlet and many coloured uniforms… the hymns sung by such a huge crowd sounded magnificent.' But Lilah was shocked to see that most of the troops surrounding the arena carried rifles. Were they armed? They were indeed, Basil told her, and with live ammunition. Military memories were long. Fifty-four years ago the Indian Mutiny had started in the Meerut while most of the English were at church.

Monday saw the polo finals and the presentation of the colours. There were more dances, sometimes two a night, in which Lilah generally ended up dancing with Gerald Stewart, and dinners in the Mess tent, where she was usually placed next to Colonel Barnes. One night the Comte de Madre dined with the Hussars 'Great was my dismay when I saw him. Colonel Barnes protected me from him the whole evening. But he managed to ask me again what ship I was returning by. He is not much liked by the army. He told me one of the men had asked him to dine because he owed him money – I think for a polo pony.' Lilah's guess was well-founded. The Comte's habit of buying favour by lending money to impoverished young officers had become well known in the Tented City.

Next morning Helen Mitford visited Lilah in her tent. She felt she should tell her that Colonel Barnes was in love with her.

The other officers looked on me as their Colonel's future wife and did not talk to me much when he was present as they thought he might not like it … all, including Helen, were on the look out for signs and every little action of mine was taken to mean something. Captain Mitford had said to Helen that he was quite sure that the Colonel was in love because he was so cross with the men and depressed and unlike himself ever since I had come to the camp – and worse, that he and all the others thought it such a pity that I seemed to ignore him and give him no encouragement.

Lilah was nonplussed and annoyed. 'I told Helen that there was no truth in the story. She must get her husband to contradict it.'

10

Durbar Day

Despite gloomy forecasts, the morning of the 12th broke fine and cloudless. Lilah woke early to the sound of bugles and trumpets, the lilt of bands and the tramp of marching troops, heralding the day around which the whole Durbar week would revolve. Lilah left her tent at 10 a.m. and travelled by car with Judy and Sylvia, parallel to the track for horse-drawn carriages. The Hussars' camp was only a quarter of an hour's drive from the amphitheatre, where they were guided to the semi-circular grandstand for 'Distinguished Spectators' by calm, rather peremptory British soldiers. Behind them were the chambers specially built for the great Indian ladies in purdah, the hidden wives of the maharajas. Some must have already arrived, for through the 200-foot-long fretted screen she could hear the hum of voices and just make out shadows and movement. Every so often a steward would gesture to the back as if to say 'Sit down – don't forget the purdah ladies.'

On arrival Lilah was separated from Judy and Sylvia and taken to the section reserved for the families of peers and maharajas (Sylvia was a baronet's daughter, which evidently did not count). Here, however, she found herself among other friends mingling with their Indian hosts. The Maharaja of Indore introduced Lilah to the Begum of Bhopal, who was with her son Prince Obaidullah Khan. 'She was covered from head to foot in gold, like a yellow chrysalis, completely enveloped in a gold yashmak with only eye-slits and a gold chain armour sort of filigree arrangement dropping from her rich crown.' Lilah had been determined to meet this remarkable woman, who was the third successive female to inherit her kingdom and had already been ten years on her throne. She spoke English well – and was also fluent in Arabic, Persian and Pushtu. She had written a book on schools for Indian women and, like the Gaekwar, was renowned for reforms in her state. But before the conversation had a chance to get interesting, they were interrupted by another English visitor.

The Durbar was about to begin. On the far side of the arena, on a curved embankment half a mile in length, was a swathe of close-packed bobbing heads, students ranged in groups from different colleges, universities and schools from every region of India, sixty thousand Indians in costumes and turbans of green and blue and gold, gleams of dazzling white, like a vast kinetic painting or the floral triumph of a master gardener. In the centre of the arena stood the Royal Pavilion forty foot high, its platform ascended by a wide marble stairway, its ceiling supported by wafer-thin gilded poles, with a canopy of scarlet velvet fringed in crimson and gold. Designed by the Director of the Lahore Art School, the pavilion was topped by a gilded dome symbolising the sun floating in a blue sky, under which two gold thrones awaited the King Emperor and the Queen Empress. Away to the left and linked to it by a long red carpet, stood a smaller *shamiana*, also of crimson, gold and velvet. It was here that the King would receive homage from the princes.

Thousands upon thousands of troops had now taken up their positions, spreading out like a fan in a wave of shining uniforms and accompanied by exuberant marching bands. Of the 100,000 spectators, Lilah's stand alone carried 16,000.

From Colonel Barnes's description of the planning of the day Lilah recognised the Royal Navy Marines on either side of the flagstaff bearing the Royal Standard. The guards of honour took up their position to the right of the dais, the 53rd Sikhs to the left. The Lancers, in bright scarlet uniforms with their green, blue and white pennons streaming above their heads, mingled with the green and crimson uniforms of the Baluchis; while the turbaned native infantry in khaki with flashes of bright orange made a dramatic backdrop to the red doublets and dark kilts of the Black Watch.

At 11.30 a.m. the sound of booming guns in the distance signalled that the King had left his camp. First to enter the arena were heralds and trumpeters on white horses, and massed bands playing Handel's 'See, the Conquering Hero Comes'. These were followed by 800 elderly men of magnificent bearing – veterans of the Indian Mutiny, greeted by a burst of cheering as they took their seats. The Viceregal procession came next in carriages and full escort, while Handel rang out again – 'The March of Scipio'.

Just before noon the King and Queen reached the entrance, heralded by a 101-gun salute. Their open landau drawn by four horses reduced its pace to a walk. At the sight of the Emperor with his Empress by his side, attended by two Indians holding over their heads a gold-embroidered crimson umbrella and a fan-like sunshade, the whole assemblage rose to its feet.

The royal couple wore the robes in which they had been crowned at Westminster Abbey – the Queen in purple velvet and white satin with an emerald and diamond tiara and the Orders of the Garter and the Crown of India. The King had wanted to re-crown himself with the original British crown in front of his Indian subjects, but this well-meant gesture had been vetoed by the Cabinet and the Archbishop of Canterbury. The Maharaja of Nabha had suggested that since the King was representative of the deity, as were, in their way, the Indian princes, a new crown should be placed on his head by three ruling chiefs – a Hindu, a Muslim and a Sikh. This, too, was vetoed. Finally, it was decided that he should make his entrance with a new crown already on his head. A foot in height, it sat on a cap of purple velvet and ermine, with a band of 6,170 diamonds interspersed with emeralds, rubies and sapphires.

The 10th Hussars turned away from the royal carriage, allowing the Noble Guards their moment to lead the long procession round the arena and down the central road to the *shamiana*. Amid erupting waves of Indian salaams and the cheers of the Europeans, another forest of colour: the Noble Guards' white tunics, sky blue turbans and glittering aigrettes, the blue-clad Hussars, the bodyguards in scarlet and gold, the shining helmets and cuirasses of the Life Guards and the Horse Artillery's embroidered yellow jackets. Alongside the King's carriage rode the dignified spotless white figure of Sir Pratap Singh. From the *shamiana*, where they had been waiting, under the control of the Indian Lord High Steward with his long wand of office, ten young pages, all princes or descendants of princes, moved forward to settle the long purple trains of the Imperial couple.

The ceremony began with the homage of the official apparatus of Colonial rule in order of precedence. First the Governor-General, the Commander-in-Chief and the Executive Council; next the Chief Justice of India in scarlet judicial robes and long dress wig, accompanied by the puisne judges of the High Court of Bengal; then the Governor-General's Legislative Council and the governors and lieutenant-governors of the Provinces; finally, with Schubert's 'Ave Maria' playing sedately in the background, those lesser provincial dignitaries who had been lucky enough to catch the eye of the authorities.

Then the Durbar sprang into life, as one by one the princes and ruling chiefs, resplendent in gorgeous clothing and priceless jewels, made obeisance to their Emperor, employing every variety of salutation. The Viceroy had ordered them to wear formal Indian court dress and display all their British decorations. They were to bow once to the King and once to the Queen and then walk backwards for seven steps before exiting to the side.

The elaborate ritual started well enough with the Nizam of Hyderabad. The King returned his bow and looked long and earnestly at him. He was followed by the Gaekwar of Baroda, second in importance only to the Nizam. The Gaekwar broke every rule in Lord Hardinge's book. Arriving at the amphitheatre in full dress and covered in the historic Baroda jewels, he removed them all just before the moment came for him to approach the King. On reaching the *shamiana*, he made a cursory bow from the waist, stepped backwards and then, wheeling around, turned his back on the royal couple and walked from their presence nonchalantly twirling a gold-topped walking stick.

There was a murmur of dismay from the crowd, but the Maharaja of Mysore and the rest of the ruling chiefs performed impeccably. From some came a gesture as of throwing earth (as though from under the royal feet) on the head, from others a simple bow, placing their hands together palm to palm, sometimes over their swords. The Rajput chiefs, bowing deeply, laid a sword in turn at the feet of the Emperor and the Empress. Most reverential of all were the chiefs of Sikkim and of Bhutan – who after bowing profoundly threw earth by gesture seven times on their heads and drew from their breasts two white shawls, used only to drape the most sacred images of their gods, to spread before the King. Lilah was thrilled to see her little Maharaja of Jodhpur leave his place among the tableau of bejewelled princes beside the throne to perform his own personal homage, repeatedly rehearsed with his uncle Sir P, placing his sword against his head and then laying it carefully at the feet of his Sovereign '...dressed in a long-skirted cassock, ruby-studded sword, armlet of precious stones and a brooch of the King-Emperor's initials in diamonds – the gift of his majesty – fastened on his turban... There was a great difference in the manner in which the various Chiefs made their bows. The nicest of all was an old man – Kashmir – in black silk and gold who kissed his sword several times and then laid it at the King's feet.' At the time Lilah had not really taken in the Gaekwar incident but she noted in her diary 'People were indignant with Baroda whose casual nod was anything but respectful – the crowd's comments were quite loud.'

At the conclusion of the homage, the King and Queen rose. Shielded from the sun by the crimson and gold umbrella, the royal couple made their way hand in hand to the sound of triumphal music along the red carpet towards the raised platform of the Durbar Pavilion. Lilah recorded: 'Lord Durham and Lord Shaftesbury walked backwards all the way facing the royal procession, which looked so magnificent and oriental. In front of the solid gold thrones their Majesties turned and stood before the assembled multitude in all the panoply of Majesty, the very air seeming alive with light, and throbbing with the sound of music and the welcoming shouts of some hundred thousand souls.' The heralds strode forward to the foot of the thrones to break the silence with a fanfare from their silver trumpets, after which the Chief Herald read the Royal Proclamation solemnly announcing His Imperial Majesty's Coronation, first in English and then in Urdu.

The King and Queen returned to the *shamiana*. The artillery fired a royal salute, and the troops blazed out a *feu de joie*. From here the King made two momentous announcements: the partition of Bengal (the least popular of Lord Curzon's measures) was to be annulled; and India's capital would be returned from Calcutta to Delhi. Lord Hardinge in his memoirs remarked that although as many as twelve people had known for six months of the change of capital nothing was leaked – 'It was one of the best kept secrets in history.'

At first hardly anyone had been able to hear the King. But Hardinge had set up a special printing camp, cordoned off by troops and police three days before the event. His leaflets arrived immediately after the King had spoken. Within minutes, word spread like wildfire over the amphitheatre.

The change of capital caused Lilah and her circle 'a good deal of sensation', but the elevation of a smaller and predominantly Muslim city to the centre of power came as a blow to Calcutta's Hindu business community. But the repercussions would come later. A flourish of trumpets and the 1,600-strong massed band crashed out the National Anthem again. The spectators rose to their feet as one with cries of 'God Save the King'. Their Imperial Majesties re-entered their carriage to another 101-gun salute and drove away from the reverberating amphitheatre to the sober quiet of their camp.

Just when it all seemed over, the people from the mound rushed down, piercing the guard of soldiers as if it were paper, prostrating themselves on the grass to catch up the earth trodden by the King and press their foreheads against the marble steps. John Fortescue, in a book rushed out and dedicated to the King, expressed the conventional Imperial wisdom of the day: 'The East has not yet lost the ancient habit of exalting their Emperor above all human kind. So strong is the impulse in men ... to pay homage to the one supreme leader of all India... to deify the power which keeps them in discipline and order; and thus brings to them the divine blessing of peace.'

As Lilah left, she noticed that the lattice purdah screen was in fact made of cardboard and had dilapidated into threads and patches as the ladies had poked their fingers through the beige card and torn holes to widen their view of the spectacle.

King George found the Durbar ceremony a wonderfully moving occasion. Once back at his camp and still in his State dress, he summoned Hardinge to his tent to express his thanks and congratulations. Lord Hardinge was euphoric. Despite having had to cut back the number of troops from 80,000 to 50,000 due to a shortage of fodder after a severe drought, he had masterminded the greatest Durbar in history – and there were still three days of celebration to come. Never before, he felt, had there been a pageant representative of so much wealth and power, of such diverse races and creeds and interests, all combining to pay tribute to the Emperor. As for the Gaekwar, whose untoward behaviour had barely registered with the King, nothing would allow the incident to go unpunished: 'During the next few days', he wrote, 'everybody was wondering what notice I intended to take of this incident. To those who enquired of me I merely said "You will see later." These words I knew would be repeated to the Gaekwar who, from my certain knowledge of his psychology, I felt sure would be getting more frightened every day by my inaction.'

That evening seventy-two maharajas and ruling princes were invited to a State dinner, dressed in their courtly attire, in the banqueting tent at the royal encampment. Taking meals in public was for many Indian princes at variance with their traditions. Those who were faithful to strict Hindu and Muslim codes of practice had accepted the invitation with the proviso that they were not obliged to enter the dining tent until the dessert, at which stage they would sit near the King but apart from the main table. No such suggestion of compromise had come from the Gaekwar, who had received his invitation in September. He did dine out in Europe, he told the Viceroy, but when in India he was in purdah.

In fact the Gaekwar was less calm than his outward appearance suggested. The first sign of the gravity of the situation came early that evening. He dropped into the tent of his friend the Governor of Bombay and received a 'not at home'. Returning to the Baroda encampment he was met by one of his friends in a state of agitation. On his advice the Gaekwar dashed off a letter to the Viceroy, professing his loyalty. He explained that owing to his nervousness in the presence of the King, he had become confused and had turned to ask for direction on how to proceed. The official world was seething with anger at the way he had behaved but perhaps this letter would be enough to repair the situation.

11

The People's Fête

Each day brought the King Emperor an opportunity to commune with his Indian subjects in a different way. The 13 December was less formal – a people's fête and a garden party in the Red Fort. Lilah put on a primrose-coloured muslin dress she had been saving for the occasion, cut square at the throat and edged in lace and silk. She added a string of moonstones which glimmered on her neck, suspended from an invisible chain. She looked dazzling.

> ... the only garden party I have ever enjoyed. It was the most brilliant affair – masses of Maharajas, Princes in full eastern apparel, Europeans, scores of men in uniforms, English ladies in exquisite hats and jewels which shone in the sun, and non-purdah Maharanees and Indian ladies in saris of every hue, all making a great glittering mêlée in the wonderful old buildings and exquisitely carved white marble of the Dewan-i-Khas. Bands were playing and fountains poured sprays of water out of the freshly mown green lawn with mounds of roses, with Muslims, Christians, Sikhs, Parsis, Hindus and Bhuddists walking and chatting together, many of them drinking champagne and smoking cigars. On the Fort's roof a *shamiana* had been put up for the Indian Princesses and ladies to watch the party. I talked again to the ruler of Bhopal. She told me she 'painted' with her needle – last year she won prizes for her embroidery at an exhibition in Allahabad. Apparently it's mainly the men who embroider in India.

Under a small *shamiana*, the Imperial couple spoke to everyone who was presented to them and then slipped away from the Fort garden into a private room, from which they re-appeared in their coronation robes escorted by their pages. Without fanfare or trumpets they walked to the Fort walls and took their place on a marble balcony – the historic site

where the Emperors had received the acclamation of the Delhi populace. Alone and remote, raised far above the crowd but visible to all,
they quietly displayed themselves. In front of them the plains stretched
away southwards into the distance.

When they saw their Emperor King and Empress Queen on the
balcony, a mighty shout arose from the crowd and flags were waved.
From all over India people had come by train or on foot for this celebration. Many of them had been standing for hours to find a viewing
position opposite the balcony. One Tibetan had travelled four months
to see the King. He started his journey back to Tibet the same night.

The air stirred, and the people's fête shook and vibrated with the
sound of pipes and music, Katora song, cymbals, bells, cylindrical
drums attached to the neck by leather straps, beskirted dancing
dervishes and Khattak sword dancing. The Maharaja of Jaipur had
brought his performing elephants; the Nawab of Rampur a circus; the
Maharaja of Gwalior his Chinese fort, built for a mock battle. There
was wrestling, tilting, kite flying; there were magic mirrors, musical
rides, jugglers, acrobats and stunning feats of horsemanship with a
troupe of Sowars leaping to and from their steeds at full gallop. All
afternoon a gigantic papier mâché cobra hovered over the Imperial
couple's head.

Arrangements had been made that after prayers in Delhi for the long
life and happiness of the Emperor, processions of Hindus, Jains,
Muslims and Sikhs would form outside their temples and mosques and
march by different routes to the Fort where their chiefs were awaiting
them. As they passed directly under their Emperor, who had travelled
5,000 miles across the sea to be with them, they would make their final
supplication for unity and peace.

From her vantage point high in the Fort, Lilah watched the arrival of
the processions with the Maharaja of Patiala, who was on the Durbar
Committee and had taken responsibility for the ambulance and medical
arrangements. He had personally brought 5,000 men from his state.
Leading the procession with kettledrums warning of the approach,
eight elephants rolled ponderously forward; they were followed by wild
horsemen in stiff gold capes, with breastplate, lance and shield. Others
were dressed in dark blue with rings of steel encircling their high
turbans and gorgeously caparisoned horses whose riders carried sacred

[65]

emblems – these were the austere and fearless Nihang warriors for whom protecting the Sikh faith from its enemies was the sole reason to exist. On a smaller elephant was seated a high priest who guarded the Granth, the sacred book (last seen by Lilah in the Patiala prayer tent) which accompanied the Maharaja wherever he went. At the sight of the priest, fifty or so yellow-turbaned Sikhs swarmed round his elephant, singing a chant with antiphonal response in ceaseless repetition, to the accompaniment of drums and tambourines.

So important was it for their Imperial Majesties to see, be seen and receive homage that for an hour they sat in serene acquiescence, their pages fidgeting by their sides as the sea of faces continued in wave after wave. The officials travelling with the King forgot the doubts they had entertained about the security and political risks of the royal visit. Faced with the astounding reaction of the people, they were taken utterly by surprise. Perhaps the King had been right after all to reject their advice to play it safe and stay in England. By the end of the after-noon half a million people had passed before them.

As dusk fell in the golden glow of ancient Delhi and Lilah joined Sylvia, Basil and Gerald to return to the camp, she felt herself inspired by the spiritual devotion she had witnessed. She wrote cryptically in her diary: 'It was an envious sight at sunset, to see the most devout Mahomedans fall down on their knees, wherever they just at that moment happened to be sitting or standing, and bow their faces to the dust, turning towards Mecca and saying their prayers to Allah.' A telegram the same day brought her back with a shock to Western life. 'News came that the King's relations, the Princess Royal, several chil-dren and the Duke of Fife travelling to Egypt had been shipwrecked off the Moroccan coast. All were now believed to be safe.'

Night came suddenly and the city lit up with the subtle subdued glow of thousands of little oil lamps. In the Maharajas' encampments, torches encased in blue and ruby glass flared and sprays of coloured electric bulbs sprang into light. The sound of music and laughter continued into the early hours. This was the first time all the chiefs had met together for eight years – since the Curzon Durbar. Gossip did the rounds. The Gaekwar of Baroda's daughter, engaged to the eminently suitable Maharaja of Gwalior, had been seen dancing all night, every night, in the Cooch Behar camp. The *on dit* was that she had fallen in love with the Maharaja's glamorous brother and might break off her engagement. Patiala's most respected doctor, a high practitioner of herbal medicine, had eloped with an English girl, though to the Maharaja's relief there would be no scandal: she was not a marquis's daughter but the *au pair* to a clerk.

The most lurid story concerned the Maharaja of Patiala himself. The famous Patiala jewel collection contained a necklace insured for the equivalent today of ten million pounds, a diamond breastplate composed of 1001 brilliant blue-white diamonds. Until the end of the century, it had been the custom of the ruling Maharaja to appear once a year before his subjects with a glorious erection, naked except for his breastplate. This was considered a temporal manifestation of the Shiva Linga, the sacred phallic form of the God Shiva. As the Maharaja walked about, his subjects' happy applause acknowledged both the dimensions of the princely organ and its radiation of magic powers to drive evil spirits from the land.

The young Maharaja, practising to emulate his forebears, had apparently taken – with mixed results – to walking nude along the marbled halls of his palace in his own impressive state of priapism, the more startling, on a good day, for being proudly sustained even when his member was festooned with ropes of the renowned Patiala pearls. The holy joy of this sacrament was impossible to share freely with the Indians' repressed Christian masters, especially the women. Basil, however, heard the story, though it was only to Sylvia that he had dared repeat it, in a watered down version. Sylvia, of course, hastened to whisper it on to a shocked Lilah.

The serious talk in the camps centred on the previous day's events. The *Times* correspondent visited ten of the camps and informed his readers that the announcement of the new capital was being received without enthusiasm. Some blamed the Calcutta monsoon, others suggested that it was a reflection of a British intention to remain permanently in India. It was believed by some that Calcutta had been chosen as the seat of power because it would be easy to leave by sea in case of an uprising (which overlooked the simple explanation that Calcutta had been the Head Office of the East India Company). Among the merchant class there was a sense of desertion. Calcutta and Bombay were the business capitals of India, certainly not Delhi. The Bengalis kept an ominous reserve – here the journalist foresaw more serious agitation. Only those maharajas embedded in semi-independent rule with the Government were pleased to have closer contact with the Viceroy in Delhi. The Rajput princes were beaming and shaking hands with each other; Sir Pratap Singh had long been pressing the case for Delhi to the British. It was the heart of Hindu territory – and a matter of pride to north India, which considered itself the citadel of India.

As for the Gaekwar of Baroda, his peers, who held him in the highest regard, were concerned. He could not have bargained for the storm that was now unleashed. The Anglo-Indian newspapers were in an uproar. The Viceroy was rumoured to be brewing revenge. Admittedly the Maharana of Udaipur, doyen of the states of Rajasthan, had not attended the Durbar, though he had been present in Delhi. But as chief of the thirty-six royal Mewar tribes and highly conscious of his clan's place in history (his ancestors had ruled long before the Mughals and had never been conquered), for him to appear bowing to the British King would have implied subjugation, and his was a special case. The King's visit to Udaipur in 1903 as Prince of Wales had permanently shaped his sentiments towards India. Moreover, this Maharana had an impeccable track record of loyalty.

Hardinge had not yet accepted the Gaekwar's letter of explanation and had refused to see him until he had made a full public apology. Behind the scenes, the Viceroy had summoned the Baroda Resident, who had confirmed his suspicion that the state was rife with sedition. Hardinge had written a secret report for the British Government mirroring the Resident's views and emphasising that since as long ago as 1905 the Gaekwar's conduct had been dubious – not only had he been unable to deal with the extremists in his state, but he had actually tolerated them in his own household. Within the week, *The Times* wrote a leader lifted almost word for word from Hardinge's report. The pressure on the Gaekwar was growing.

Meanwhile Lilah was in a carefree mood. The next three days were crammed with dinners and ceremonies, at which, to her relief, the Hussar officers at last stopped treating her as Colonel Barnes's property. His loss was their gain. They were free now to speak to her whenever they wanted. On the other hand, being genuinely devoted to him as a man and a war hero, they were disappointed for him that there was no truth in the story 'as they thought I would have made such a splendidly suitable wife for their Colonel, which I was much flattered to hear'. She thought – she certainly hoped – that the high level at which he moved in political and military circles protected him from being aware of the gossip. Anyway, now that the most important events were over he was far less tense. He adopted a tone of light-hearted teasing, even exchanging practical jokes with her (she raided her wardrobe and sent Basil to the Mess dressed as a woman: the Colonel retorted by instructing her ayah to wake her at 5 a.m. for a non-existent review.)

On the morning of 14 December, Sylvia and Lilah set off to watch the King's military review at the polo ground.

> The part that I enjoyed most was our Hussars, who galloped past at full tilt in a cloud of dust, and also the seven-year-old Nawab of Bahawalpur with his 220-strong camel Corps. In full uniform of khaki and gold-embroidered skirt, he sat in front of his camel's humps, servant behind, with a sword as big as himself when he saluted. Then, equally delicate and alone, came our little Maharaja of Jodhpur, who rode a beautiful white Arab with a gold saddle cloth at the head of his troops looking very proud as his sword flashed in the sun. Just before he made the salute, his horse swerved away from the waving plumes of the King's entourage, but without taking his eyes for a moment off the King, he brought it full square to the front and completed his salute before charging off like lightning to a roar of applause from the crowd.

That evening Lilah went to the King's camp for the State Investiture. After the glamour and excitement of the Indian and troop ceremonies, these proceedings seemed to her pompous and interminable as hundreds of British and Indians received their honours from the King. After the official investiture, the Viceroy rose from his place on the King's right, bowed to the Queen and led her out of the tent. In an ante-room she put on the robes of a Knight Grand Cross of the Star of India and the Viceroy led her back into the tent, where the King kissed her and invested her with the Order of the Grand Star of India. Almost immediately, a cry went up of 'Fire!', the electric lights flickered and dimmed and Lilah heard the piercing sound of fire whistles outside.

Close to the Reception pavilion a tent belonging to the Foreign Secretary's aide was ablaze and was rapidly being pulled down. Alarm spread among the three thousand guests. Lilah began to leave her seat but Hardinge shouted 'Sit down! Nobody is to leave his place.' The King and Queen did not move and news soon came that all was under control. Luckily there was no wind. The cause had been a messenger's bicycle lamp leaning on the canvas.

As soon as she could, Lilah returned to her camp to join Sylvia, Basil and Gerald in the Mess tent. 'After dinner we played games and fooled about. We form an inseparable quartette now; it is such fun, wherever we go we are together. It is a curious fact that Gerald is exactly the same age as I am, twenty-three, and that we are all four Irish.'

Next day, two miles from the centre of Delhi, a ceremony took place which had appeared on no one's schedule, the inauguration of New Delhi as India's capital. In front of a small crowd of five hundred people in a spot below the Ridge, predominantly ruling chiefs, the King spread mortar with a gold trowel on dressed stones ordered secretly from a Chandni Chauk mason, lowered into position by a pulley and made into a plinth. To loud applause the Maharaja of Gwalior offered to give the plinth a statue of the King Emperor.

In the afternoon came the Military Tournament and a point-to point. The 'quartette' watched the proceedings together, with Lilah close beside Gerald and spellbound by the camel race: '... a most dangerous sport involving the animals being pushed as hard as possible towards the jump made of solid mud seven foot high.' In the evening came the last dance: 'Gerald and I danced together most of the night until 2.30 a.m. and Gerald thought he was in love with me, but I told him it was only moonlight and romance and the spell of the East.'

12

Farewell to Delhi

On 16 December the Hussars were again lining the streets for the King's departure, along the same route as the State Entry. Troops were again deployed to ensure the King's safety as he passed through the potential danger zones. This time the cavalcade would proceed at a trot, with the procession lasting less than an hour, and the Chiefs would not be on show – the King would be receiving them earlier in his camp, where he would dispense more honours before bidding them farewell: 'Colonel Barnes says that the King has made several stupid tactless mistakes, speaking to some of the Maharajas and ignoring others. He is very worried, as he realises how our hold on India depends so much on this Durbar and the effect it will have on all these great ruling Chiefs.'

Having had enough of public displays, Lilah took a last opportunity to visit the carpet shop, Schwaigers, in the Chandni Chauk, with Lord Iveagh. In the darkness at the back of the shop, behind the heaped rugs and carpet rolls, she could just make out a trader squatting on the floor in front of a low counter. Among the coloured rags in his cheap tin travelling-box he unwrapped for her an astonishing collection of gems, necklaces, charms and rings. Lilah bought far too much. In the distance she heard the final royal salute of 101-guns firing from the Ridge as the royal party entered the Fort.

The King and Queen were received at Salemgarh station by Lord and Lady Hardinge. There they parted company. The Queen went south to tour India, while the King departed to go shooting in Nepal, where King Prithvi had died five days earlier from cirrhosis of the liver. Tense diplomatic exchanges had followed with the Nepalese Prime Minister. Much political capital had been invested in the visit and King Prithvi had insisted from his deathbed that King George's holiday should go ahead as planned. Besides, he felt he had earned the right to a tiger shoot and some respite. They settled on shortening the period of mourning, rushing through the investiture of the new King and pitching the royal camp in the jungle where fifty miles of new roads had been cut for the royal shoot.

Returning from her shopping expedition for lunch at the Mess, Lilah's heart sank. Letters from England had arrived. She could barely make herself read them. 'It all seems so very far away now, and I seem to have lost interest in the news people tell one from home. I am entirely engrossed in the life out here. It is rather awful that I have become so wedded to India.' The worst of it was that she and Sylvia would be parted. Sylvia had been invited to Calcutta and would delay her return home for several months. Lilah was leaving next day for Peshawar and the North-West Frontier with Judy and Arthur. 'This is the wind up of everything. The Great Durbar week is over ... oh how sorry I shall be to end this camp life and say goodbye to all the friends we have got to know so well – it feels to me like home here.' This was more than a passing regret. The freedom and laughter of the last fortnight had been a rediscovery of the happiness and independence of her childhood in Ireland. There was, however, a back-handed consolation: '...plague has broken out in Delhi, and although there are only a handful of cases so far the Viceroy has planted plague officers everywhere. Also, smallpox is increasing, with several cases in the camps, so perhaps it's just as well we are leaving...'

There was a strange atmosphere in the Tented City. With twenty-four hours to go, people were starting to say their farewells and the camps were closing down. Sir John Hewett was selling the furniture by auction; except for the furniture of the royal tents, which was offered for sale by private arrangement. The city's dismantling and closure was the culminating triumph of organisation and economy – within a week not a tent would be seen standing, the site returned to farming or wasteland.

To relieve her unhappiness, Colonel Barnes invited Lilah for a final excursion, dutifully chaperoned by Judy: 'Obtaining a car somehow, we travelled 15 miles to see the Qutub Minar, the famous huge high tower and ruin. We climbed 350 steps to find a glorious view of all the surrounding country with Delhi in the distance. A few yards on we found wells, eighty feet deep or more, which Indians dive into for a rupee.'

Colonel Barnes tried in vain to encircle a strange old iron pillar with his arms, his back against it. According to tradition anyone who succeeded would have their wish granted. His eyes were sad. They both knew that the gesture was a mute acknowledgement of unrequited longing. 'All around us lay the curious flat country, the site of ancient Delhi, covered by broken walls and ruined Hindu temples, a soft pinky glow from the setting sun lying on the old walls. We looked for ancient remains and antiquities among the rocks.'

They drove slowly back, ruminating on the extraordinary fortnight they had shared. The Durbar had been for Lilah less a political event than a glorious pageant. As a child of her time, she believed in the civilising power of Britain. For her the Empire and the social order were as indestructible as laws of nature. Yet she was not at all spoilt. The simplicity of tent life had brought a sense of reality to what would otherwise have felt to be impossibly extravagant and self-indulgent. Nor did she share the assumption of superiority that afflicted many of the officials of the Raj. She was too Irish for that. In the maharajas she saw equals, not subjects. Her brief experience of India had revealed this contradiction, but she had no more idea than far wiser heads how to resolve it.

With his knowledge of the security arrangements and his experience of conflict on the North-West Frontier, the Colonel knew a lot about nationalist unrest and was far more conscious of the fragility of the Raj than most of his brother officers. He spoke admiringly to Lilah of Hardinge's Durbar, which had been a colossal triumph: 'He told me that those who had been at the previous Durbar said that nothing in Lord Curzon's time could match last week's proceedings – in spite of there being no elephants and that the State Ball was not held in Dewan-i-Khas ...' But he was profoundly relieved that his responsibility for the King's protection was at an end. Troop deployment was regularly reassessed at the daily briefings in the Government headquarters: '... the officials are much more afraid for the King's safety in Calcutta than they were for him here, as the people are so much more seditious there ... some of the natives refuse to think that the real King is in India at all. They say he would never have trusted them enough to come and that this must be some man acting as the King's double – there perhaps lies a great part of his safety, for they would not bother to try and assassinate a substitute.'

The last 10th Hussar dinner, on 16 December, was outside, with a concert and an enormous bonfire which everyone sat round as the soldiers sang songs. Lilah was deeply moved by the evident affection of the soldiers for their Colonel: 'We all joined in the singing, Gerald Stewart of course sat by me! Colonel Barnes got up on the platform and made a short speech praising his men for the splendid way in which they had done the hard work of the past week and he was cheered and cheered and they sang "For he's a jolly good fellow" so loudly that tears came to the eyes.'

Lilah's tears were also for Gerald: 'He is going on a shoot with Basil then has to return to the Cavalry School, which he hates … I had to bid him a tender farewell as we are starting at cockcrow tomorrow to catch the 7.15 train.'

13

The North-West Frontier and the Khyber Pass

Lilah rose at 5.30 and took a dark, chilly breakfast in the Mess tent with Judy. Despite their early start they barely reached the station in time. The roads were chaotic, as if Delhi were departing *en bloc*. Pushing through the crowd on the platform, they found Arthur anxiously waiting beside the train. He hurriedly dispatched their luggage with porters, and escorted them to their four-berth ladies' carriage, where to their dismay three strange women were already installed. The sleeping arrangements would be tricky unless one of the intruders got out before nightfall.

The carriages on the Peshawar train were older and distinctly less comfortable than those on the special Bombay–Delhi train. As they rattled through the flat, barren land a plague of yellow dust, combined with soot from the coal-fired engine, penetrated the cracks of the windows and doors. Lilah's clothes, hair and every inch of exposed skin became 'utterly filthy'.

The train stopped for a few minutes at a series of small stations, allowing Lilah just enough time to dash out and buy pieces of meat or bread from itinerant native vendors and stallholders before rushing back to her carriage, where Judy would be anxiously holding open the door as the train pulled away.

Their first proper meal came at Lahore, where they entered the large fortified station through a tunnel protected by loopholed towers and turrets. 'The army turned a lot of buildings into strongholds after the Mutiny,' Arthur explained as they joined him in the refreshment room for first-class European travellers. Lilah liked its air of extravagant splendour and its somewhat dissonant Anglo-Eastern style of decoration.

Returning to their carriage, they found to their relief that the three strangers had left the train. There was room now for Judy's maid, who had been having an appalling journey travelling third class. At each stop she had uncomplainingly ministered to her mistress, but as the train became more packed she had grown increasingly distressed, sandwiched in her carriage amongst a horde of ayahs and Indians with no wash room. In the short stops, at wayside stations, the guards would not accept delays. Some women queuing for the privacy of the platform lavatory had been left stranded. Those who had not dared risk missing the train were obliged to use a corner of the carriage with a hole in the floor, protected from view by sympathetic ladies holding up their saris as a screen. Judy soothed her distraught maid, ushered her in to their first-class compartment, bolted and barred the door and windows and closed down for the night. However much they banged and knocked, she was allowing no one in.

Next morning, as they approached Rawalpindi, Lilah saw a series of gigantic sandhills, broken by rainstorms into a myriad ravines and crumbling into fragments in every direction. With so few signs of vegetation there were no clues as to how the scant flocks of goats could hope to survive. The line then passed through a few short rock tunnels to emerge into level country – dry and parched still but with glimmers of green and a wider view. 'It looked a desolate out-of-the-way place,' Lilah wrote. 'I don't wonder none of the 10th appreciates being quartered there.'

The last hundred miles took seven hours. Lilah watched with mounting excitement as the spurs of the Himalayas began to push towards them. The air became colder and the land more lush and irrigated as they drew into Peshawar, known to those familiar only with the colonial sector as the fairest of towns, full of shady avenues and a wealth of flowers. 'This isn't India; it's central Asia,' Arthur said as he joined them on the platform.

They were to be guests of the Chief Commissioner of India's North-West Frontier Province, Sir George Roos-Keppel, who had entertained Lilah during the Durbar. They reached Government House, a long low building some way out of the cantonment, to find sentries pacing up and down outside. A very tall crimson-liveried Indian servant with a long knife and a revolver stuck into his belt (whom Lilah recognised from Delhi as one of Sir George's bodyguards) led them to an ADC, who told them apologetically that their host had been very ill with pneumonia. He was on the mend, but under doctor's orders to remain in bed. At dinner they met other guests, including Michael McKenna, brother of the rising Liberal politician Reginald McKenna, and John Spender, the editor of the *Westminster Gazette*, said to be the best-informed Liberal newspaper in England. Spender had the latest gossip about the Durbar from London, where an 'almighty row' was brewing about Baroda's and Udaipur's 'snubbing' of the King – *The Times* was on its imperialist high horse supporting the Viceroy, while most Liberals were sympathetic to the maharajas or thought it at worst a storm in a teacup.

Lilah's objective was the Khyber Pass, a mountain station of the ancient 4,000-mile Silk Road from China to the Mediterranean and one of the few passable routes from India to Afghanistan; it was here that the opening action of the Second Afghan War had taken place in 1878. But she would have to wait. Travel there was only possible on Tuesdays and Fridays, when the pickets would be on guard to protect the caravans crossing the border from Afghanistan. Any other day would be too risky. As an added precaution Sir George would be sending a special protection squad with her on Friday.

Her movements were restricted even in Peshawar. 'No woman would dream of going about unarmed or without a man, as the natives are a very murderous lot and would stop at nothing ... raids made by the outlaws from the mountains mean extra precautions for safety have to be taken against this fierce and savage people.'

With a Government House bodyguard she walked into the native part of the city which had 'a character all of its own... with its flat-roofed mud houses and, beyond, range upon range of rocky mountains, white-tipped with snow and very beautiful'. She found the independent mountain tribes 'a much wilder and more Asiatic-looking people than at Delhi – paler complexioned, Jewish-looking, rather like the types supposed to represent our Lord in Bible pictures'.

More powerfully than ever the feel, smell and music of India capti-vated her '... in the market there were dark-skinned men squatting on the floor, at work in the most primitive fashion with a potter's wheel and some brown clay – the different shapes of the pots and vases they made forming as if by magic under their hands ... and nearby herds of camels resting, their bales being unpacked by Afghan traders who had travelled over the Pass bringing wares from Persia and Afghanistan into Peshawar.' She tried exploring the British sector, but its suburban blandness and uninspiring public places had no meaning for her. The zoo's collection consisted of a bear, a tiger, one bird, five monkeys and a few very ordinary guinea pigs and rabbits; and it was the wrong time of the year for the desolate scrub that called itself The Gardens.

Outside the town a team of French archaeologists was excavating among ruins and ancient walls and pillars. They had recently caused a sensation when they discovered an urn supposed to contain the bones and ashes of the Buddha, and Lilah watched in fascination as they lifted more and more enigmatic, earth-encrusted objects from the dust.

At last came the day she had longed for. On 22 December they set off to try and reach the Fort at the edge of the Frontier, on the borders of Afghanistan – the farthest extreme of British territory. 'The people', she wrote, ' are never allowed to go beyond a fort eleven miles lower down, Ali Musjid, as if they do not leave the pass before dusk, the pickets and sentries are withdrawn and then casualties occur. As a rule no risks are taken but with Sir George's special permission we can go to the furthest point and the pickets will be kept out on the mountains to guard the pass until a later hour just for us – which will make us feel very special.'

Before sunrise Lilah set out in a tonga, protecting herself against the bitter cold in a thick coat with wraps and rugs. Judy and Arthur went separately. Their guide and protector was Captain Maffrey of the Khyber Rifles, accompanied by an orderly carrying a loaded rifle.

All the heights of the mountains on either hand were guarded by armed sentries, who saluted as we passed nearer and nearer into the heart of the blue rocky mountains towering overhead and seeming to close in upon one in a threatening manner. We wound up the steep rocky path, crossing herds of pack-laden camels and hordes of weird Asiatic-looking tribes of Afghans, Bhutans, Tajiks, Afridis and other native traders, some seated on small furry donkeys and brown mules or bullocks, all passing down into Peshawar on these caravan days, down over the Khyber Pass into India. As the sun rose, it turned the distant snow-capped peaks into dazzling glory, range after range, all blue and white and gold but no greenness anywhere or vegetation of any kind – just rocks and dry steep heights, with here and there a tiny stream of water crossing the rocky road. When we reached the first fort, Jamrud – a long mud-built wall of fortifications – we changed into two-horsed tongas, which went twice as quick and in which we rattled along in fine style, Mr Brodrick and Judy in one, and in the other I was seated with the native orderly whom Sir George had sent with us.

The exhilaration of the adventure, the contrast between genteel tea party life at Government House in Peshawar and the death-ridden narrow track on which she now found herself, filled Lilah with energy and fearlessness.

The lean-looking little horses from Central Asia which are used in these mountain tongas in Northern India are wonderful beasts. The sharp stones and the steepness of the road seemed not to affect them one bit as they cantered up the steepest parts and trotted serenely down the rockiest paths. At one point we got the most wonderful vista of what lay behind us from the heights we had already scaled – the Vale of Peshawar, bathed in the early morning sunlight, a veritable promised land, all barrenness hidden and obscured. It was ten miles from the fort of Jamrud to the fort of Ali Musjid but we accomplished it within an hour, rough climbing though it was. We had been particularly told by Captain Maffrey that we ought if possible to pass the second of these two forts not later than 11 o'clock. Crowds of different tribes from the heart of Asia tramped along in bands at intervals on the road. One rather dangerous lot of Afghans we were told were escaping from the Amir of Afghanistan as he had tried to force them to work without pay.

Clouds of dust raised by passing camels filled Lilah's eyes and ears, mouth and nose. She was too engrossed in her surroundings to care. As they passed a large rock, caravans of Muslim travellers coming towards them stopped to do homage to it. The rock was said to bear a mark from a kick from the Prophet's horse when he had ridden through the Pass 1,300 years ago. Around the next corner they came to Ali Musjid, where worn battlements stood on the flattened top of a pyramidal hill sandwiched between high mountain ridges, the site of the first battle of the Second Afghan War, in which the 10th Hussars had been engaged. Captain Maffrey gave them a graphic description of the conflict, pointing out the exact place where each soldier had fallen. Lilah pictured the scene as if it were happening under her own eyes – the wounded and dying men, the shots and ambushes behind every curve, the confusion and sniping and desperate rescues. But they could stop only briefly at Ali Musjid, having to press on the eleven miles to the last British outpost of Lundi Kotal.

They reached the mud fort and descended stiffly from their tongas. A detachment of the Khyber Rifles posted outside the walls saluted them and the commander, Captain Hume, a tall man with a keen strong face, received them. For six months without a break – always on the watch for frontier trouble and in total isolation – this bleak garrison would be his headquarters, until he was relieved by another officer. He escorted them up the steep hill called 'Pisgah' (meaning 'extensive view') with an armed squadron of a dozen natives. Below them was the borderland of India and Afghanistan, and beyond that the road to Kabul and Central Asia, a route taken by few Europeans, for none could travel safely. Over the distant snow peaks, the mountain country stretched into infinity.

Over lunch in the Mess at Lundi Kotal, Lilah found herself deeply moved by the unassuming courage of the officers:

> ...such fine virile men. I watched them as they ate and compared their lives and their uncomplaining harsh life for their country under such isolated and uncompromising conditions with the lives of our pampered easy-going Guardsmen in London, who would have made a shocking fuss at being even banished to Pirbright or Aldershot! and here were these men – officers in the Army too – serving the same King and yet never thinking about the hardness of their position or their lack of luxury or their longing for home and friends and sport such as other men could indulge in – but setting themselves to their tasks with cheerful serenity and a

[80]

humble diffidence about themselves and their powers which marked them out to my mind as true men.

Under strict orders they left at three o'clock so as to be out of the pass by dusk. 'The journey home and the change of horses at Jamrud, the sun going down over the tops of the mountains at the entrance to the Pass was something I shall never forget.'

14
Face to Face with the Mutiny

Two days before Christmas the trio set off by train on the next stage of their tour, south-east to Rawalpindi (known to everyone as 'Pindi'). They arrived to find a sprawling encampment which quartered several regiments. Colonel Barnes had returned from Delhi with the 10th Hussars and would be their host once more. With many of the officers on Christmas leave, he installed them in the Mitfords' house – a typical Anglo-Indian bungalow with an elegant verandah leading to a large jasmine-scented garden. All night long a guard patrolled outside.

During that week Colonel Barnes continued to press his claims with Lilah, entertaining her with tennis and dinner parties and each morning delivering a beautiful chestnut horse to her front door. Lilah's riding nerve had returned: 'I rode for miles and miles each day in a lovely wooded park.' She was thankful for the temporary escape from the unrelieved Britishness of a military outstation and the guilt induced by her relationship with Colonel Barnes.

On Christmas Day, after church and carols, they ended the evening talking and laughing round a blazing log fire with no other light. Colonel Barnes snatched a moment of intensity: 'I had a serious talk with him in between the others' chatter. I do like him very much but …'. The Colonel had enlisted Judy as his confidante and poured out his heart as far as his English reserve allowed. Judy reported: '…apparently I had such a snubbing manner and never met a man half way… I had rather be accused of that than the reverse and I don't want to meet him half-way!'

What the Colonel failed to realise was that what he offered her could never be enough. It was India, not Anglo-India, that she wanted. Wherever she went invitations to stay longer were pressed upon her '… I almost wish people wouldn't ask me to things that I can't possibly do, when I want to so dreadfully.'

Not without difficulty Lilah found Pindi's native town, some way from the military quarters. She rode into its centre, where the White Mosque rose up gloriously pure against the blue mountains and sky. 'In the market, laid out on the ground amid the noise and dust, were carpets, rugs, carved boxes, embroidered bedspreads, and all manner of things, whose skeletal owners importuned us in the wily and persuasive manner known only to an Eastern trader ... fifty rupees for two gorgeous silk embroidered tablecloths, made in Kashmir, with the most lovely colourings, one with mauve flowers on a pale champagne-coloured ground, exquisitely worked ....'

The last evening before their departure the Colonel came to say his goodbyes. He stayed for an hour and with a meaningful look at Lilah said he would be in London on leave in the summer. But her thoughts were elsewhere, on her impending long journey across India.

Lilah set off next day with Judy and Arthur, in the pitch darkness of an icy dawn. The zigzag route they had planned made Lilah feel they were sight-seeing 'à la yankee', but she was determined to visit some places fast and furiously rather than not see them at all, for she knew in her heart that she would never return. At Umballa Station they were joined by a friend of Arthur's whose battalion was quartered in the town. He had taken leave and had arranged to spend the next week with them. Even with all the windows shut, the dust somehow managed to force its way in: 'the yellow powder covered everything and I felt I had been eating and breathing dust for days as my throat and nose were lined with it when I woke after taking an afternoon nap – it was also tiresome having to drink one's tea without milk in it and eat toast without butter but it is supposed to be unsafe to touch either at any of these small stations in India.' Twenty-four hours later, 300 miles south-east of Delhi, they arrived at Lucknow, 'the Constantinople of India', the cultural and artistic capital of the silver age of the Mughal empire, also known as City of the Nawabs after the Persia-loving Shia Nawabs of the city. They settled into Wutzler's Royal Hotel, bathed, changed and gave their dusty clothes to an ayah.

It seems so odd our four rooms near together, opening on to the same verandah, just as if we were married couples. It is rather fun being two and two, and Judy and I feel just like two married couples travelling alone, only we can't decide which husband belongs to which. I am going to wear a wedding ring I think for the benefit of the people in the hotel ...

They spent the morning resting. After lunch the four of them sat on the verandah bargaining with the numerous itinerant traders who were squatting in the sun and laying out their jewellery, embroidery and curious *papier mâché* work on the brick floor.

An ancient patriarch with a very black wrinkled face and nothing on but a sort of towel wound round his body showed us some marvellous conjuring tricks – or rather feats of magic for it would be an insult to call them anything else but magic. He made my ring disappear and reappear in a marvellous fashion and he did that renowned trick of Indian magic, which no one has ever been able to discover how it is done – to make a mango tree grow from a seed under one's very eyes in two or three minutes. He then produced some snakes and a mongoose from various small sacks and we witnessed a fight between them – the mongoose came off victor and killed the snake.

Restored by their visit, they hired a carriage to drive round the city and its gardens, redolent of a history of courtly manners, poetry and music. Their destination was the Residency, which had been at the centre of the notorious siege in the Mutiny, but Lucknow's glorious domed skyline brought a pang of regret at the shortness of their stay.

The pile of ruined buildings in the sunset, with clumps of gorgeous crimson bougainvillea making a rich note of colour amongst them and the green graceful palm trees as a background, were very peaceful and beautiful, and it was hard to imagine the bloodshed which took place there in the Mutiny not so long ago. An old veteran who had been actually through the siege of Lucknow, an eyewitness of the whole proceeding, showed us round and by his graphic descriptions made every detail live again for us just as it was in 1857. He pointed out to us the actual spot on which the gallant Sir Henry Lawrence met his death by a shell which pierced the walls of the Residency, wounding him mortally. We visited the cemetery and saw his grave which bore this inscription 'Here lies

The State Procession with the Red Fort ahead

Maharajas and their entourages passing lines of troops at the State Entry

The Maharaja of Jodhpur aged 13 with his political adviser by his side during the State Entry

The King Emperor makes his State Entry into Delhi on his small horse

The King Emperor with his Queen Empress in the Royal Shamiana during the
Durbar Coronation

The Begum of Bhopal with her eldest son, Prince Obaidullah, attending the Durbar

The Gaekwar of Baroda whose behaviour at the Durbar scandalised the Viceroy

The Gaekwar of Baroda turning his back on the King Emperor

The King Emperor and Queen Empress receiving homage from their subjects on the historic marble balcony at the Red Fort

Gerald Stewart, captain in the 10th Hussars, who fell in love with Lilah

Looking for antiquities among the rocks outside Delhi

Lilah (right) with Colonel Barnes, chaperoned by Judy Smith

Lilah visits Delhi's famous shopping street, the Chandni Chowk

The King and Queen departing from Delhi after the Durbar

Sir Henry Lawrence, who tried to do his duty. May God have mercy on his soul!' and all the other monuments raised to the memory of the men who were killed in action or died from the awful effects of the siege, which lasted four or five months before relief came ... I picked a little rose which grew close to Sir Henry Lawrence's grave and I have pressed it and mean to keep it as a relic. At Cawnpore we shall see still more remains of the Mutiny – the well down which the awful Nana Sahib in his treachery threw the victims of his massacre and the famous so-called Blood Steps, which they say no British soldier ought to look at, as it over-excites their animosity against the native of today.

On the evening of New Year's Day they set off by train for Benares – India's sacred Hindu city. With only a day to accomplish everything, they booked in to Clarkes, a small and charming hotel with verandahs sheltered by palms and dew-laden roses placed lovingly on their breakfast table.

They drove to the river and boarded a primitive boat to watch semi-naked Hindus, men and women, bathing in the Ganges, praying to their gods and to the sun, and afterwards drinking the filthy disease-ridden water in a timeless Indian performance of a ritual that had been enacted over the centuries. They saw the Burning Ghat, a part of the river's bank set aside for the cremation of corpses: the bodies were laid on piles of faggots and then set alight. What remained was thrown into the river. 'There are a lot of holy men here, identified by their long hair and the curious marks on their arms and foreheads – a red vertical line just over the eyebrows meaning they are dedicated to Shiva, the many-formed god of destruction, procreation and delight.'

Afterwards they hired a carriage and drove out to see the ruins where the Buddha used to preach – '...a vast pile of reddish coloured brick and stone, marvellously preserved considering the centuries which have passed since Buddha came out from Benares with his disciples and preached his first sermon from the heights of this tower'. After a brief supper in the hotel they caught the night train to Lucknow, where they arrived at 5.30 a.m. They had a breakfast of toast and tea in the waiting room and within the hour took another train for the short journey to Cawnpore.

Booking one night at the pretentious Empress Hotel, the four set off in a carriage to find The Memorial Well, the scene of one of the worst atrocities of the Indian Mutiny, now marked only by gardens, an unkempt wall and a handful of religious memorials. To this day, there are differing accounts of the events of June and July 1857, when a besieged, starving British garrison was assured of safe passage by river to Allahabad if they surrendered, but was massacred as the soldiers tried to float the boats stranded in the shallows. The men were all hacked to death and the surviving women and children imprisoned in Bibi-ghar, a small house run by a prostitute. As a relieving force approached, the prisoners were murdered with meat cleavers and their bodies thrown down a well. The British responded with savage reprisals of their own.

Lilah learned the story from a Gordon Highlander who gave her a graphic account of the slaughter.

He described how the followers of the Nana kept two hundred women and children shut up in that awful small space, in the heat of an Indian July, for fifteen days and then sent butchers to cut them to pieces after the Sepoys, on being told to shoot them, refused and fired into the air instead. One felt all the bloodthirstiness of revenge rise up in oneself, even after all these years, and I can imagine well how the rescuers who came too late to prevent the massacres simply let their vengeance have no bounds and 'saw red'. No punishment seems too great for such gruesome barbarous butchery, even that which they administered to the half dozen or so of the Nana's followers whom they succeeded in catching – namely to make them go into the scene of the late slaughter and lick the blood from the floor, which horrible though it was, was more degrading and awful to a Hindu as it destroyed their caste, and then had them hanged on what was to them a sacred tree, near by.

We saw the actual tree, close to the well, guarded by rails. The most lovely gardens have now been made all around this once terrible scene and there is a memorial plaque on which is inscribed the long death-roll of those who fell in the siege and during those few days of the massacres. We then drove a few hundred yards further, to the edge of the river, where the Nana's most treacherous act took place – when he gave the English prisoners permission to embark and go off safely but then as soon as they got into their boats ordered his sepoys to fire on them, unprotected as they were. Now the Ganges flows by, mistily grey and shimmering in the sunlight and the 'blood steps' as they are called, heading down to the water's edge, are covered with 'dhobies' – men and women washing their clothes and beating them on stones to dry, singing cheerfully to themselves all the while.

Lilah found it hard to sleep after her day in Cawnpore. Images of Vasily Vereshchagin's vast war paintings of India kept coming to her. His works were passionately anti-British. Soldiers were forbidden by the military authorities to visit his exhibitions – his most famous painting, *Blowing from the Guns*, implied that executions carried out by tying sepoys to the barrels of guns were standard British practice. That was untrue of course, but what was true was that the Mutiny had seen terrible acts on both sides. Lilah kept her thoughts to her diary and said nothing to Arthur or Judy.

15

The Taj Mahal by Moonlight

Their next stop, after a day's train journey, was Agra – above all to see the Taj Mahal, the marble monument to his favourite wife by the love-struck Emperor Shah Jahan, who also built the Red Fort in Delhi. Lilah was deeply moved by its beauty, which she looked at with the observant eye of a watercolourist, and like many women before and since she was drawn to speculate on the Queen who had inspired it.

They three drove off from their hotel. After dinner they went again to see it by moonlight. Lilah's description is of a Taj Mahal as yet unspoilt by mass tourism, standing apart from the world, in a sacred silence of its own.

We drew up at a huge dark archway in shadow and stepped out of our carriage and walked through the doors, escorted by two natives with lanterns, and then suddenly there burst upon one's view the most gloriously lovely view of this world-famous building… It seemed hardly possible that it really could be a building of man's work, it seemed more like some delicate fairy fabric…. The moon overhead was quite full and the air wondrously still and warm and scented and as we stood there spell-bound the silence and mystery and beauty charmed one into feeling there could be no reality about it all, it must be a dream and one felt one could not speak except in hushed whispers. All around lay the lovely garden, with long tree-bordered paths, silver in the moonlight, romantic alleys which ended in dark nothingness and sheltered corners where were placed white marble seats and where one sat and looked and looked at the scene before one and felt as if one could never look enough… As if one could not come away, the place seemed to draw one and keep one there, and though I can well imagine in daylight the whiteness of it all and the gold-topped dome must be almost too dazzling and blinding, at night it was softened into dim purity of outline and the very beauty of the architecture was enhanced by the marvellously softening rays of the moon. The indisputable but strange fact is that for all its immense size it looks so very light and delicate – as if it might easily float away. We wandered about and mounted the flights of marble steps and gazed at the River Yamuna below us as we stood on the topmost terrace and penetrated into the innermost recesses, between screens of carved white marble of such exquisite workmanship that they literally looked like the finest lace. And beneath the vaulted domes there lay side by side the two tombs, one of the Shah Jahan, the maker of all this loveliness, and the other of his wife, the Queen, who requested her husband on her deathbed to raise such a tomb to her memory as would be the wonder of the world... the monument of one man's love for one woman – the Eastern expression of his grief at her loss and his wish to perpetuate her memory – just a woman's tomb – that was all.

For nearly a century, from the time of the scholar and conqueror Akbar the Great, Agra had been the capital of the Empire. Akbar built the seventy-foot-high crescent-shaped Red Fort, whose somewhat uninviting walls, moated and bastioned and a mile and a half long, contained a hidden paradise inside, created by his grandson Shah Jahan when he converted the Fort into a palace. Lilah spent most of the day in this massive citadel, with its Pearl Mosque, its gardens, its audience halls and its smaller palaces, but as the afternoon wore on she was unable to resist the lure of the Taj Mahal. She returned to it at sunset.

... more wonderful than can be imagined. We stayed gazing at it in silence, till the glow disappeared entirely and gave place to soft pearl grey when the tints of the marble changed to yellowish ivory and all colour and life departed from the scene... The echo within the dome is marvellous, when one raises one's voice, it echoes and reechoes on, a long ringing note of sound, for several minutes. The smell of incense and the hot still air within adds to the solemnity and hushed awed feeling which steals over one on passing through the carved marble screens which enclose the two tombs where the dust lies of Shah Jahan and his Queen.

Lilah was now captivated by the story of Shah Jahan and his family:

> especially beautiful among the palaces which the Emperor Akbar
> and his grandson Shah Jahan built was the palace for the Queen,
> inlaid with precious stones, agate, lapis lazuli, turquoise and
> cornelian in brilliant tracery. One could imagine this favoured,
> beloved Queen lying on her marble couch, on the narrow marble
> balcony with its wonderfully carved screens and looking over the
> river below to the blue distance beyond, hazy in the heat of the
> sun... one wonders whether she loved her Emperor as he must
> have worshipped her and whether she was stifled with all the
> costly splendour and magnificence with which he surrounded her.

Sylvia was due shortly to rejoin them from Calcutta and after three
weeks spent mainly with Judy and Arthur, Lilah was longing to see her
again. With a few days to kill they visited the Itmad-ud-Dowla, on the
bank of the River Yamuna, the exquisitely inlaid tomb of the father of
Nur Jahan, the powerful Persian Queen who effectively ruled the
Mughal Empire after Akbar's death during the reign of her weak
husband Jahangir. But nothing could compare with the Taj Mahal, and
Lilah was left unmoved.

There was still just enough time for some sightseeing in the countryside before Sylvia's arrival. They decided to make their base in
Fatehabad, a native township outside Agra, staying at a posthouse –
one of many simple bungalows all over British India kept up by the
Government for travellers: '...beautifully clean, with flat wooden
bedsteads, or charpoys as they are called, and a table and chair or two.'

Wherever they went Arthur discovered an inexhaustible supply of
army friends, or friends of friends, with access to rickety cars and with
bearers to carry their picnic baskets and their guns and cartridges. En
route to Fatehabad, followed by a couple of officers and their native
servants, they planned to rendezvous at a small village, from which the
men would go on a shooting expedition. When the car behind Lilah's
failed to turn up, Arthur sent their own driver back towards Agra to
locate the inevitable breakdown and rescue the passengers. A crowd
immediately materialised, staring curiously at the white strangers,
'every woman carrying a fat naked baby, Indian style, on her hip'.
Before long, the husbands ordered the women to go back to work in

the fields, leaving the men 'to resume their indolent lazing about'. With her iron constitution, Lilah was impervious to stomach upsets and willing to try virtually anything that came her way. She sucked sugar cane and ate 'rather dirty' butter balls, chapattis, red chili pepper and slices of coconut provided by the villagers.

It was her first taste of real native food and she did not enjoy it. Eventually the car returned with its cargo of apologetic officers, who sent on the lunch to the posthouse. As this was not far away, Lilah refused a seat in the car and accepted the offer of a ride in an *ekka*, 'a shaky and very uncomfortable little two-wheeled conveyance' pulled by a pony in which she wobbled unsteadily to her destination.

After lunch the native police lent them scraggy but very agile police horses on which Lilah and Judy rode astride on men's saddles into 'flat country, dry sandy soil with deep gullies filled with thorn bushes, down which my horse climbed like a cat'. Birds and animals were everywhere:

….wild peacocks and fascinating green parrots, grey doves and green parakeets and jackals and every now and then a wild mongoose scuttling away. Sometimes shikaris and coolies ran by the side of my horse, and would stop and point ahead and I would see a herd of black buck … we met two shikaris carrying a dead buck slung on a pole between their shoulders. I feel so marvellously well out here that it is a joy just to be alive and in the country and in India with the sun shining!

Next day they returned to Agra and visited the spectacular tomb of Akbar, grandfather of Shah Jahan, which he had designed for himself and started to build while he was alive. 'He and his grandson are entirely responsible for all the beautiful buildings in and around Agra. He also is said to have invented a new religion which he called Divine Faith …a man of very independent thought, wonderful in those faraway days of fear and superstition.' Lilah was right about Akbar's liberated way of thinking – he was tolerant of Hindus to the point of indulgence and was feeling his way towards a universal religion incorporating the insights of all faiths. But in the hands of his followers it turned into a hero cult and soon failed.

Sylvia joined them in Agra on 8 January, the day the King and Queen left for Bombay to catch their ship home. Knowing it would be Sylvia's only chance to see the Taj Mahal by moonlight, Lilah rushed her there off the 10 p.m. train from Calcutta. 'Without any warning a vivid flash of lightning behind the trees under which we sat lit up the whole gloom and intensified the black effect of the trees against its brilliant light – it was an awe-inspiring and rather terrifying sight ... to watch the effect of an Indian thunderstorm over the Taj Mahal. The thunder and lightning continued all the evening and very heavy rain fell which laid the dust.'

After ten minutes, Sylvia pleaded to go back to the hotel, complaining of tiredness after her twenty-four hour journey.

> I stayed talking to her till nearly one o'clock. She would not let me go ... she had a most wonderful time in Calcutta and had been presented to the King on the polo ground. The pageants, she said, made the Delhi ones seem pale by contrast... The Indian people were ecstatic with joy to see their Emperor... . The Bengalis had never been combative people, they did not struggle desperately like the Rajputs and fall back into their deserts sooner than yield their independence. The Nawab of Murshidabad, in the most lavish costume she had ever seen, was the star, wearing an enormous flat engraved emerald on his right arm, a historic talisman, leading a procession ... trains of camels and horses in sumptuous trappings and elephants drawing a gilded carriage containing court poets and literary men... .

The show Sylvia had seen had been meticulously planned in London by Messrs James Pain and Sons, but as at the Delhi Durbar it had been completely taken over by the panache of the Ruling Chiefs. Lilah was sorry to have missed it – but she had seen wonders enough herself and there were more to come.

16

Jaipur

They jolted and shook in a simple country train westwards to Jaipur. Lilah and Sylvia shared a small cabin with hard wooden berths facing one another. Judy and her maid were next door, and Arthur and his army friend further down. They arrived at Jaipur station at five in the morning, were shunted into a siding and allowed to sleep there for two hours before making their way to a primitive little bungalow on the edge of the city calling itself the Jaipur Hotel. Within minutes a courtier from the Maharaja of Jaipur appeared on their verandah to invite them to the royal palace the following day. Despite being held up in Delhi, Thakur Dhokal had made all the arrangements.

This was Lilah's first experience of living in an India free – or relatively free – of the British presence. Admittedly an avuncular Resident was in place in manorial grandeur who paid weekly calls on the Maharaja. But the Maharaja's loyalty, tested over his thirty-year reign, appeared unquestionable and their meetings were mostly taken up with the exchange of pleasantries. Certainly, the Government had seen no need to remove the Maharaja's control over civil and criminal law or his power to pronounce the death sentence.

Jaipur City was surrounded by massive walls, within which sandstone houses lined exceptionally broad intersecting streets of hewn stone laid out by an enlightened eighteenth-century Indian maharaja and his architect in the form of a classical Roman grid. Some sixty years before the Durbar, the entire city had been painted pink to honour the arrival of the then Prince of Wales for a tiger shoot. For a while, Lilah sensed something different about the city that she could not quite put her finger on. Then she realised what it was – the absence of the sanitised order of a territory run by the British: no policemen on the roads; open drains everywhere; the only car that passed belonged to the Maharaja's household. As she walked among a stream of humans ceaselessly on the move and clad in every colour under the sun with elegant saris and small

Rajput turbans, she felt the warm intimacy of animals crowding in on her – camels, bulls and bullocks laden with burdens or pulling carts, stumbling into gas lamps. In the City centre she came across a five-storey building shaped like a honeycomb – the Palace of the Winds – with hundreds of small porthole windows inset with grills, finials and domes. These were designed to give royal purdah ladies the opportunity to look out, thoroughly screened, into the market place to watch royal processions.

> I always knew Rajputana would be the most fascinating part of India. ... the native dress more vibrant than I have yet seen ... snake charmers abound, with their flat baskets of live cobras and curious flutes on which they play to charm the snakes... . The peacock and the pigeon are sacred here and are not allowed to be killed. In the city are flocks and flocks of blue pigeons and soft little grey doves with pink heads, they settle in swarms all over the queer pink and yellow buildings in the bazaars and sit too on the backs of the oxen and goats which lie about in the sunny streets in undisturbed serenity.

With Sylvia she found a shop selling enamel work – 'fascinating objects, chains of garnets for which Rajputana is famous, lovely uncut gems – all the things in which my soul most revels ... jade and turquoise necklaces, one of lapis lazuli, in a wealth of blue colour, caught my eye – and held it alas!'

Lilah was somewhat obsessed by precious stones. The Maharaja of Jaipur, Sawai Madho Singh, had been a glamorous figure during the Durbar week, when he had worn some fabulous jewels in the procession after the State Entry – a necklace in three tiers of rubies the size of pigeon eggs and on his chest three enormous emeralds. His ancestors' most valuable treasures were buried in the hills above the city, guarded from generation to generation by a warlike Rajput tribe. Once in his lifetime, each Maharaja was allowed to visit the site to select the jewels that would embellish his reign. Rumour had it that Sawai Madho Singh had visited the cave where the hoard was kept just a week before the Durbar.

The Maharaja's invitation was not to the honeycomb building but to Rambagh, a few miles out of Jaipur, which had been transformed into a pleasure palace. In three courtyards there was room for nine wives, with their names on the door for convenience. The Maharaja, who lived in the fourth courtyard, could enter any apartment without any of the other queens knowing.

His father had been inspired to build the Jaipur Art School for the education of craftsmen and women by the Crystal Palace exhibition of 1851, where he had displayed pieces specially commissioned by the British, from artists of his State. Sawai Madho Singh had continued the tradition and now there were exhibitions throughout India of Jaipur's spectacular enamelwork, jewellery and miniatures. He was justly proud of this, and also of the recognition given to his All India People's Famine Fund during Durbar week and of the King's bestowal on him of the honorary rank of Major General.

Even so, for all his good work, Lilah found his charm as disquieting as that of the Maharaja of Indore:

He has five wives now and eighteen concubines, but no son which is a profound grief ... we walked with His Highness in his garden among great clumps of jasmine all over the place, palm trees and cactus plants and little temples with gods inside. We were taken to a deep pool where bits of high meat were thrown in to make the alligators and turtles rise for our inspection – we thought proba- bly the Maharaja feeds these odd pets with his cast-off wives when he has tired of them... .

The Maharaja lent Lilah a horse and an escort, a Dutch captain called Van der Gucht from the Jaipur cavalry, who showed her the Royal stable with the famous dancing horses she had seen at the People's Fête in Delhi, which seemed almost human as they pranced, knelt and bowed at the captain's command. They rode to an enclosed park where tigers, black panthers, monkeys and every kind of duck, crane and stork were on view.

The following day the Maharaja sent one of his best elephants to meet them for a dawn excursion to Amber Fort, the State's former capi- tal, a few miles north of Jaipur. On the main road stood the monumen- tal wise animal covered with scarlet trappings and led by a mahout in a brilliant green turban

... an animal truly worthy of its master the Maharaja. It knelt for us to climb into the howdah – Sylvia and I one side, Judy and Mr

Brodrick on the other while Capt Van der Gucht knelt on the beast's back and held onto the rail of the howdah. It only held four but as there were five of us he had to cling on behind as best he could. Two guides with magnificent yellow turbans walked beside us ... the huge beast swayed us around from side to side and going up the steep hill it was difficult not to slip off backwards before the top. ... Just before the sun got fully up, there was a blue mist over the tops of the hills and a sort of fresh indescribably sweet smell everywhere, a mixture of jasmine and incense ... Peacocks with gorgeous colouring sat on ruined walls and old yellowish gates half tumbling to pieces, with cactus leaves concealing the broken arches, and pomegranate trees with red fruit hanging on the branches climbed up little dome-topped temples, in which some Hindu deity of marble or stone was enthroned ... a lovely old ruined palace and fort on the heights of the mountain before us, and beyond a lake in which it was all reflected – a blue vista of hills and valleys lying still further in the distance.

They left for Ajmer next day at two in the morning. There was not much chance of sleep in the rickety train, but the resourceful Arthur Brodrick discovered that for six annas an hour they could keep their carriage in Ajmer station all day, using it as resting-place and luggage depot before catching the night train. Shunted off onto a siding they made a leisurely start at 8.30 a.m. and breakfasted on 'somewhat dubious' eggs and coffee in the waiting room.

They took a gharry, a horse-drawn carriage shaped like a palanquin, up a hill above Ajmer and gazed all around them at range after range of blue, steep, rugged mountains; they looked down onto a lake, the Ana Sanger, where white marble palaces rose up from the water's edge, 'the sun glinting through their dazzling pillars – straight marble columns tinted with golden gleams' .

Then on into the native city to a ruined Jain temple, now converted into a mosque and came across

a patriarchal old priest – a veritable Aaron he might have been – with long white garments, white turban, long white beard. ...White pigeons fluttered about, and a native squatting in true eastern fashion under an archway was baking chapattis over a tiny fire... After that we went to a shrine – Dargah – one of the holiest in India, to which Mohammedan pilgrims daily come from far north and south. The inner shrine of all – a lovely little carved white marble mosque built by Shah Jahan – we were allowed to enter but it was guarded by massive silver gates which on special occasions are opened to pilgrims, to allow them to take one look within this sacred spot.

There was time for one last expedition seven miles away into the Aravali hills. By the sacred Pushkar lake they were surrounded by monkeys with grey furry faces springing from tree to tree with their babies clinging on to their tails. Then down the narrow rocky pass and as dusk fell, they reached the station and their waiting railway compartment with only minutes to spare before the train set off south-eastwards to Udaipur.

17
Udaipur

Lilah woke to her twenty-fourth birthday at Udaipur station. Two pairs of little brown ponies conveyed their tongas at a hectic gallop to their out-of-the way hotel, 'clean, quiet and cut off with scarcely any visitors because it entails quite long journeys to or from anywhere'. They found a shady corner of the stone courtyard with a view of the mountains and distant lakes and after so many nights snatching sleep in trains, they rested at last 'limp and tired in easy chairs, with books and cushions and sunshades and everything that the heart could desire'. Letters had arrived with birthday greetings and complaints from Lilah's mother of influenza and the fraught political situation in England, where after a summer of strikes 'landlords, peers and monopolists' had been identified as the class enemies of the unions. 'At least we're not monopolists,' remarked Lilah, who wanted no reminding of how little she looked forward to returning home and how brief a time was left for her in India.

The Maharana of Udaipur sent Lilah's group a handwritten invitation to visit two of his palaces, apologising that he could not escort them personally on their 'far too short' stay – he had affairs of state that he had to attend to urgently. Thakur Dhokal had told him that the Jaipur visit had been a success – he hoped Udaipur would be equally enjoyable. The concierge of their guesthouse had a further suggestion – would they first like to see an Indian harvest festival in the centre of the town? Lilah had no difficulty in persuading Arthur to accompany her. Sylvia and Judy, still complaining of exhaustion, would take the tonga and join them in a couple of hours' time.

The four-day festival was in full swing and Lilah was soon caught up in the swirl and gaiety of the crowded streets. The spice-laden air – cardamon, turmeric, ginger, coriander, chilli, cumin – hung in the heat like a veil; animals claimed equal space on the road with men, women and children; camels grunted along, sucking in breath, lowering the flap of their bottom lip with an expression of dismissal; donkeys, carrying huge loads, moved in a cloud of flies; a cow covered in bells and bright cloths nosed into Lilah as it made its way through the throng, led in a clumsy swaying dance by a man on either side. For the next four days the sun would be in transit northwards to Capricorn to meet the tropic at the time known as Uttarayan, when the Gods wake up from six months' winter slumber. Prayers all over the town were being offered to the Sun God and to Saraswati, the Goddess of Knowledge.

The house fronts were hand painted with paste of vermilion and orange in complicated symmetrical patterns. Steered from the roof terraces, kites criss-crossed the sky in dramatic dips, darts and sweeps. Lilah saw small groups of boys playing an ancient game with seven pieces of marble and a ball, while a musician with a pumpkin-shaped headdress went from house to house playing a long-necked lute, telling stories and chanting poems in rhyming song. Bards declaimed compositions of ritual devotion praising the gods; and people came to them with rice or money or some small gift. Lilah was stirred. The beat of the street music – entirely free of western melody – was entrancing. But the rituals made no sense to Lilah and she gave up the attempt to understand them. 'Do not worry, lady,' said the guide, 'merely to observe the rituals will ensure you a secure place in heaven.'

Afterwards they walked to a point where a flight of stone steps led down to the water's edge to find Judy and Sylvia waiting. 'A most Venetian scene lay before our eyes… All the palaces and houses had steps to the blue still water of the lakes. The Maharana's boat with a strange straw roof lay moored to the nearest island. Another boat brought by a naked brown boatman with a coloured scarf about his waist came alongside for us and we got in and were rowed across to see the Maharana's palaces on the far edge of the lake.'

A courtier took them round:

They reminded one more of Italy than of anything Indian. Inside his state bedroom there was the most gorgeous bed all made of solid glass with gaudy hangings of brocade and the richest crimson velvet. His Eastern taste showed itself also in the curious paintings on the walls of the main state apartments – peacocks, elephants and a supposed painting of himself shooting impossible

[99]

tigers in an impossible jungle – all mixed up together – regardless of perspective or colouring. But *nothing* could detract from the dazzling purity and symmetry of the white marble pillars on the paved courtyards, interspersed with graceful palm trees, through which the glorious vista of blue sky and lake was visible. This Maharana is the highest native prince in India, he would have been Emperor, I believe, had India not come under British rule, and his palaces and that of his Queen here on the edge of this lake are *too* lovely for words.

All Lilah's previous conceptions of the summit of India's romantic beauty fell away under the spell of Udaipur:

high rocky mountains seeming to guard in the peaceful lakes dotted with islands, on which lie the glorious white palaces, domes, arches, pillars and minarets all dazzling in the hot sun and reflected in the blue stillness of the water which laps up against their marble walls. …There were cranes, storks and peacocks and all manner of strange water birds… Palm trees and half-hidden palace gardens throw a speck of green colour in the scheme of white and blue.

At sunset they landed on a thickly wooded island at the far end of the lake. Navigating their way through the trees and bushes, they came out into an open place where scores of wild pigs were sleeping in the sun, before their evening feed. As they arrived the Maharana's men were dragging out sacks and scattering corn. In a trampling rush a crowd of fierce-looking boars with murderous tusks and baby pigs running beside their mothers poured out from all parts of the island, kicking up clouds of dust. The pigs were kept by the Maharana for tiger fights, with the pig generally getting the better of the tiger, Lilah was told.

That night Sylvia and Lilah lay with their door open onto the verandah, 'in spite of Mr Brodrick's entreaties that we shouldn't do so, with his warnings as to natives, to say nothing of mad dogs or jackals coming in. A large party of Americans arrived from Bombay spoiling the peace of the lovely place which we have had all to ourselves, so I am not sorry we go on to Bhopal tonight .'

Bhopal: the name evoked in Lilah an intense curiosity about its remarkable Ruler, the Begum, the only female Chief in India. They had met all too briefly at the Durbar, and had been drawn to each other. Now they would spend time together. Perhaps the Begum would unveil herself. Lilah was nervous at the prospect.

18
Bhopal

There had been rumour of plague in Bhopal, but nothing was going to deter Lilah from visiting the Begum in her home State. For two nights and a day they endured another wearying train journey, at the end of which they were met by Sylvia's friend, the glamorous Captain Amir Ahmed '...very handsome to behold, with wonderful clean cut features and sleepy Eastern dark eyes.' Captain Ahmed was the private secretary and confidant of the Begum's second son Prince Obaidullah Khan, who had befriended Lilah during the Durbar.

The Captain drove them the two miles to the Begum's guest house in his Model T Ford. 'Her Highness' would see them later in their stay. Meanwhile her carriages and staff were at their disposal and he personally – it would be an exquisite pleasure – would look after them. They were greeted at the door of the low white building by a crowd of servants, who led them to the verandah to breakfast on coffee and hot buttered toast.

Over the next week Lilah lived as in a dream. With Sylvia and Arthur (but often without Judy, who was under the weather), they were mysteriously conveyed through the streets of the town, where white bulls laboriously pulled carts, or out on the arid track roads of the countryside alive with butterflies, wild fowl, black buck and the whisper of panther and cheetah in the scrub. On the branches of the roadside trees 'uncanny-looking animals like furry bats hung by their tails'; they learned that these were flying foxes. Accompanied by an enigmatic servant in Bhopal livery, who rode with them in the carriage and attended to their every need, they visited the Mosque, the Fort and Bhopal's own Taj Mahal. In the royal parks and gardens they walked through glades of melon, lime, orange and red-fruit-clustered pomegranate – which native boys picked from the trees for them as they passed. Never knowing what they were to see, where they were to go or whom they were to visit, they surrendered to their fate. 'Whenever we reached our destination, some spell or shyness made us forbear to ask but to await events until they happened – all our movements seem like adventures from the Arabian Nights.'

In due course, Captain Ahmed came with two cars to take them to Prince Obaidullah in his lakeside palace high above the town. The Prince's wife was in purdah. Even the Captain had never seen her unveiled. By repute she was exceedingly beautiful, but no man other than her husband was allowed to know this for certain.

The Prince was fatter than Lilah remembered, with 'dark coarse skin and black beard.' Popularly known as 'Colonel Sahib', due to his rank as commander of the Bhopal Lancers, '...he looks fifty but I was told that he was only twenty-eight.' He received them for tea in his large drawing room, but with his limited English the conversation was halting and Captain Ahmed had to do most of the talking. After an hour the Prince indicated that he would like them to meet his wife, Shaharyar Dulhan. Leaving Arthur and the Captain behind, he led Lilah and Sylvia to the waiting car.

The Princess lived in a smaller palace close by. She came out onto the steps of her garden verandah to meet them.

The daintiness and beauty of the little creature simply took my breath away, accustomed as I was to the hideous old women one sees in the bazaars in India. She was of a pale olive complexion with finely formed features and the most glorious deep soft eyes with long dark lashes, under which she looked up at one with a mixture of childish curiosity and shy fear that was most attractive. She wore loose-fitting trousers of purple and gold material and little black shoes. The upper part of her was shrouded in a gauzy white sari, embroidered with gold thread, which covered her head but left visible the lovely shape of her forehead on which the dark waves of her hair lay smoothly. A rope of emeralds and pearls around her neck and several diamond bracelets and rings gleamed through the white veil and a strong smell of scent pervaded the atmosphere where she stood. ... What a wasted life for these purdah ladies. But not to them, because they find their purdah no restraint I believe, and hate it when they are forced by travelling to come under the observation of the world. But to us it seems an awful existence to be shut away and know of no life outside. She shook hands with us in turn and presented to us two tiny boys of about 3 or 4 years old with solemn faces. The eldest child, a girl, lived with the Begum, her grandmother, which was the custom for the next heir. The Princess is younger than me by several years but she was married at 13!

After introducing her sons, the Princess looked up at her husband as if for further instructions. She spoke little English, but

looked on with shy interest while we admired her boys and commented on her beautiful jewels. When England was mentioned she brightened up immensely and said she had been there with her husband last year for the Coronation and how much she had enjoyed it. She told us that her eldest boy aged 6 could speak English beautifully and she sent for him from his lessons with an English governess and sat proudly by while this funny fat child (whom I recognised as one of the King's pages at the Durbar) spoke a few quaint stilted sentences that he evidently knew by heart.

When they took their leave, the Princess gave each of them a tiny bottle of perfume from the table by her side and then with a graceful smile shook hands again and watched them go down the steps and out to the garden.

The Prince, now joined by Captain Ahmed and Arthur Brodrick, drove them to the other side of the lake to a more imposing-looking palace belonging to the Begum. Her autobiography, had recently been published by John Murray and it described the harrowing years before she succeeded to the throne. The previous Begum, at first an exemplary ruler, had fallen under the spell of a viciously ambitious man, a member of the ultra-religious Islamic Wahhabi sect, whom she had married after the death of her much-loved husband. This evil stepfather poisoned his wife's mind against her daughter, infiltrated his men into key positions, appointed himself Minister of State with despotic powers and plotted to usurp the throne after his wife's death. The British Political Adviser, alarmed at the arrogation of power and dissipation of State funds on anti-British propaganda and the destruction of Bhopal's religious harmony, took action to expose the Minister's maladministration, with great tact and deference to the besotted Begum.

In this Shakespearean drama, the daughter, into whose presence Lilah was about to enter, eventually triumphed. Her mother worshipped her second husband to the end, but even she came to realise that her State would have been ruined had she not been guided at every stage by the Resident, and in the final crisis by the Viceroy himself. Mother and daughter were never reconciled, but the dynasty contracted an unswerving, almost filial, loyalty to the Raj. When the new Begum succeeded in 1901 at the age of forty-three, she was determined to transform her country into a productive modern economy modelled on the England that she so admired.

She was waiting for them in a detached building beside her palace. They were led up a flight of stone steps into a small dark room, with plain coconut matting on the floor and a few chairs. 'The tiny imposing figure with her thick grey veil enveloping her body (and its mysterious slits through which her piercing dark eyes looked at one) rose, gravely shook hands with us and pointed to seats. For a few minutes there was an awkward pause. We murmured some platitudes to break the silence. Once this was done our hostess began to talk in very fair English and completely put us at our ease.'

Lilah had struggled with purdah ever since her arrival in India. Spellbound by the Begum, she yearned to remove the barrier that separated them. She could not bring herself to say so directly, but the Begum sensed it and gave the faintest signal to the Captain, who promptly took Arthur Brodrick by the arm and retired with him to another room.

No sooner had the men departed than the Ruler lifted her veil and Lilah saw her face for the first time ' ... ugly certainly, but beaming with intelligence and kindness. Conversation now flowed without that obscuring veil between us.' The Begum told her that the social fate of Indian women was generally dictated by their husbands – her late husband had never advocated strict purdah and since his death she had lived less and less in seclusion from the world. Her two elder sons each made their own choice about how their wives should live. Prince Obaidullah, for example, as Lilah had seen, always kept his wife in the Zenana, the women's quarters. Something in her voice told Lilah that this decision was not entirely to the Begum's liking.

A third son, Hamidullah, aged fifteen, was away at college. The Begum called for an awkward-looking, shy girl of eleven and introduced her as Hamidullah's wife, Maimoona Sultan, who had been married since she was five, when she was taken from her parents by an emissary sent by the Begum to the North-West Frontier to forage for a suitable Pathan bride. Maimoona, granddaughter of a King of Afghanistan, was the product of this mission. The Begum disapproved of early child marriages, but felt there was no alternative if she was to find a girl whom she could personally educate. Although a ceremony had taken place between her son and this infant when they were both little more than babies, she would not let them live together as a married couple till her son was eighteen, when Maimoona would have reached puberty.

The 'old lady', as Lilah called her (she was in fact fifty-three), now called for Prince Obaidullah's child. 'She explained to us that this shy round-faced little girl, with dark eyes so like her mother's, was being brought up with her so as to learn the ways of a ruler from her Grandmother, for in due time she would be ruler herself. The one immense grief of her own life was when her two infant daughters had died, as the state has nearly always had a woman for its ruler. At her death, her eldest son will rule, but Bhopal will again have its accustomed female ruler in the direct line when her granddaughter succeeds.'

After a decade on the throne, the Begum's reforms in irrigation, public works, the judiciary and medicine were bearing fruit. Her current priority was education. She had opened several new schools for Muslims, but it was the special school for Hindu girls opened four years ago that was preoccupying her at present. It had to be independent of her influence since Hindu religious needs were different from those of Muslims – and in her eyes education divorced from religion was valueless.

The more they talked the more she impressed Lilah: 'The Begum is much more advanced in thought and ideas and civilisation than other native rulers in India – her efforts for educating women and reducing the strictness of the Zenana and providing new interests in the lives of her fellow creatures without violating the ancient Mohammedan customs show her to be exceptionally wise and gifted.'

The Begum now spoke of Prince Obaidullah: 'When I assumed the reins of government, decline and decay in the army was a source of profound disappointment' she told Lilah. 'It pained me beyond measure to find luxury and indolence the chief objects of military life.' She had opened an officer training school, but after some years of unsatisfactory results she made plans for Obaidullah to take control of the army. The Rulers of Bhopal had emerged from an unbroken line of Afghan warriors and her son had the fighting qualities of his tribal ancestors.

He had proved his courage during her pilgrimage to Mecca in 1903, when her caravan was under the protection of the Turkish Sultan. 'Her palanquin, her travelling kitchen and her retinue of a hundred camels were guarded by the Bhopal Lancers, with the Turkish troops forming an outer ring until they halted for the night and threw a cordon round the camp. Sentinels were positioned at 10-yard intervals, armed to the teeth with belts of fifty cartridges and loaded carbines and remaining on watch until dawn.'

Lilah was entranced. The Begum continued her story. 'Suddenly shots rang out. Concealed in the hills, Bedouins were firing on them: unless a large sum of money was handed over to the bandits they could not guarantee the Royal caravan's fate. The Begum was reluctant to close the door on negotiations, but Prince Obaidullah was having none of it. He went into action with the Turks, assigning a detachment to protect his mother before commanding the soldiers to scale the hills and scout among the crags to discover the Bedouins' hiding place. The Begum had a narrow escape as bullets flew past her, but eventually the bandits were routed.'

When the Royal caravan halted on the hills above Bir Ali and the valley came into view, with Mecca below, 'a mysterious mild perfume pervaded the atmosphere, refreshing her innermost soul. Silence settled upon her, awakening indescribable emotions of the awe and majesty of the Prophet and the Holy City.'

On her return from Mecca the Begum had made her son Colonel-in-Chief of the Bhopal Imperial Service Troops. She wanted his appointment to be both an instrument of internal reform and an opportunity to defend the Empire and display his family's loyalty to the Crown. She had her wish. In 1906 the Prince became ADC to the Viceroy Lord Minto, and in 1908 Lord Kitchener, on a visit to Bhopal, recorded the 'excellent leadership and high efficiency of the State troops in musketry, signals and manoeuvre'.

Aware that she was encroaching on the Begum's working day, Lilah rose to her feet: 'I was so sorry when I realised I should take up no more of her time ...I have seldom passed a more interesting two hours in conversation with anyone than this wonderful old woman.' They arranged to meet again in two days' time.

Prince Obaidullah drove them home, concentrating – a little too overtly – on Lilah. He invited her and Sylvia to ride his horses next morning. His stables held over sixty beautiful animals and several ladies' saddles and he would make sure the Captain arranged an escort for them. After breakfast two bays were led up to the guesthouse by a handsome Bhopal Lancer mounted on an Arab pony. They set off with their new protector, again entrusting themselves to the dream-like world to which they had been admitted.

They trotted along hard rocky roads and dusty plains covered with palm trees and boulders. 'No fields, no grass tracks ... here and there a green patch by a native village of straw huts, where flax and rice flourished, the blue flax flowers very lovely in the sun.' Then they were led through a small wood into a luxuriant park, the grounds of the Royal summer palace.

At the entrance to the little palace our escort signalled us to dismount, which we did as in a trance, wondering what was coming next. Our fine-looking dark-skinned friend dismounted himself and threw the reins to a waiting attendant, who held Sylvia's and my horses and showed us with much diffidence to the cool shady verandah, where we were evidently meant to rest. So we acquiesced and threw ourselves down in easy chairs. He then left us for a few minutes and returned bearing two little bouquets of roses carefully tied together, which he silently handed to us each in turn on a palm leaf. He then bowed low and brought two chairs out down below where our horses waited, indicating to us to mount again, which we accordingly did and continued our way.

Each morning after their rides, the two young women would find Captain Ahmed on the verandah waiting to help them dismount. Each day brought something new. On one occasion he drove Lilah to see inside Sadar Manzil, Qaser-e-Sultani and Noor-us-Sabah – the Begum's three main palaces – and to see her again afterwards. The furniture was simple, with none of the brightness Lilah had seen in the princes' apartments at Jaipur and Udaipur, except for a blue and gold brocaded fan above the royal bed and a magnificent silver inlaid palanquin.

In a small chamber apart from the others lay a rare relic. Last summer the Begum had travelled to Europe for George V's coronation, using her visit to investigate potential improvements for her state. On her journey home she had stopped in Istanbul to visit the Sultan, with whom she had forged a lasting relationship after her pilgrimage to Mecca. He told her of his wish to ennoble her with his Empire's highest award. But the British Government instructed her to decline: only the King could confer honours on his subjects. Undeterred, the Sultan conferred on the Begum a greater honour, a gift of one of the hairs from the Prophet's beard. As a devout Muslim, she was overwhelmed. Once a year, on the Prophet's birthday, she would bring out the sacred object for display.

On the fourth morning the Captain brought an invitation from the Prince. He wished the ladies to dine with him that night. In England they would have had a chaperone, but this was India and another world. At seven o'clock, leaving Arthur and Judy behind, they drove in a sumptuous closed car to another palace. The Prince and Captain Ahmed came down the steps to meet them, ' ...in their evening dress, a simple long dark frock coat buttoned high at the throat and tight dark trousers and white turbans.' They dined in a cool marble paved room, waited on by silent bare-footed black Kidmatgars. The centre of the table was covered by a handmade cloth from Benares craftsmen 'a design of peacocks with spreading tails hand-embroidered in silver and gold and jewels ... It seemed strange to me that the Princess knew nothing of her husband's visitors but was in the strictest seclusion, and that she took no role in the gorgeous palace – these servants were no part of her life.'

Despite the small size of the party, they were greeted with thirteen courses of exquisite Indian dishes, none of which Lilah dared to refuse. With the sympathetic presence of the Captain on her right, she felt easily able to cope with Prince Obaidullah's somewhat heavy advances: 'I thought him an endearing character, a mixture of candour, simplicity and regal dignity. For him war was a natural gift, a sort of art to be perfected by iron application to study and practice ...but he seemed almost childishly pleased when we admired the crimson roses on the dinner table and glowed with pride when he told us how he had kept the Queen supplied with flowers from his garden daily during the Durbar week.'

Leaving Sylvia talking to the Prince, Lilah turned to Captain Amir. She felt herself captive to the magic of her stay in Bhopal, which was so much the creation of this fascinating man. It was a culmination of her quest for acceptance into the intimate and authentic heart of India.

The Prince interrupted them to talk of big game hunting, for which Bhopal was famous. But Lilah had eyes only for the Captain, who was telling her of the panthers which made raids into the province. Only yesterday one of them had come to the borders of the palace garden and killed two goats. Gazing into Lilah's eyes, he suggested that she should take care at night if her bedroom verandah door was left open – he had an alarming vision of a panther stealing in and eating her up. She replied flirtatiously that so far nothing more alarming than mosquitoes and a mouse had made their entrance.

In her diary she wrote:

The hospitality that the Indians lavish on their guests makes one feel ashamed for our English mode of entertaining and courtesy – I hate to think how their generosity is imposed on by many of our fellow countrymen who come to India with a big idea of how they can treat mere 'natives' and use their money for their own amusement and invite themselves as the guests of some Prince or Rajah and stay on indefinitely, accepting all the hospitality offered, as if it were their due and without any thought of returning it. Many of these contemptuously termed 'natives' are far finer truer gentlemen than many an Englishman. I loved the innocent delicacy in which the captain hinted that Colonel Wilson had telegraphed to Prince Obaidullah's office the other day, summarily demanding that a tiger-shoot should be arranged for Lord Masserene and himself, who intended to come to Bhopal and wished all arrangements for their amusement to be made. But I am glad their 'cool' order met with a check as Prince Obaidullah was away at the time and the telegram followed him round, till eventually, when it did reach him, it was too late. But all this I learnt from them and drew my own conjectures, not as if they would show me what cheek these Englishmen had exhibited but rather to reveal how sorry the Prince felt that he had through no fault of his own been unable to comply with their request.

As the thirteenth course came to its end, the Prince and the Captain rose and led the way back to the drawing room. Captain Ahmed accompanied them home in his own car. Sylvia pleaded tiredness and retired to her room but the evening was not over yet. Smoking cigars late into the night, the Captain began to talk more indiscreetly, first about his week in Calcutta helping the Viceroy with the King's visit, then about Prince Obaidullah and his brother. He was concerned about the dangerous rivalry developing between them. Hamidullah was usurping Obaidullah's position as the Begum's favourite. He foresaw trouble. The young boy was associating with 'unsavoury students' at the Muslim university in Aligarh and espousing the Caliphate movement, which was allied to the Turks and hostile to the British. Not, he added, that Obaidullah was perfect himself – he had a diabolical temper and it was, to put it tactfully, very convenient that his princess was permanently in purdah.

As he was leaving Captain Ahmed mentioned that he had been anxious for Lilah's safety. 'He told me there had been much plague in Bhopal and that it was now raging in other parts of the country close by. The English governess of the Begum's little granddaughter had it very badly, so badly that her grave was dug! But she did just recover, after they had given her up for dead …'

Next morning a car arrived to bring Lilah to the race track to inspect the Prince's horses. He had promised her that she could drive a pair of beautiful ponies which he had bought in England last summer and had won prizes at Olympia.

On Lilah's last day the Prince and the Captain laid their farewell plan at her feet. A liveried servant appeared in a Cadillac to drive her, with Arthur and Sylvia in tow, to a new lake on the far side of the town.

Two picturesque boatmen in the blue and gold Bhopal livery rowed us out to where Prince Obaidullah and the motor boat awaited us. Once all of us were seated, he took us at lightning speed to the island a couple of miles further up the lake. The boat was a new toy – no less than 66 horse power. He got it in England last year and told his secretary to have the fastest possible motor boat in existence made for him! It fairly cut through the water – I've never been at such a pace.

As they neared the island Captain Ahmed came into view, waiting for them with a sumptuous tea spread out on a carpet on the grass, complete with chairs, tables and attendants. After tea, another rowing boat came up, bringing guns and cartridges. Indicating these with a careless wave of the hand, the Prince invited anyone who liked to have a try for wild duck. Arthur Brodrick took up the offer and was rowed off towards the marshes.

Sylvia and I sat apart and watched the Captain and the Prince …the way they walk with lithe grace, and the stealthy noiseless tread, more gliding than walking, with that inimitable gracefulness of movement and poise that marks the East from the West. …The sun went down at the head of the lake, and the water all round was dyed every imaginable shade of colour. The mystery and charm of India impregnated us both and we felt as if we must breathe in the joy of this land – a land to be happy in and if circumstances allowed to drink to the uttermost both of joy and of sorrow.

Arthur Brodrick returned having been unable to get within range of any duck, but proudly displaying the snipe he had managed to shoot instead.

We got into the motor boat again. This time the engine refused to work and after several fruitless efforts we got into the rowing boats and were rowed ashore. I bade goodbye to Prince Obaidullah with profuse thanks for all his kindness and hospitality and drove home in the darkness, the wondrous starlit sky beginning to shine above our heads, and below the crickets chirruping loudly in the swamps, and the hot still air alive with insects and almost oppressively scented.

After dinner they left with the Captain for the station in two carriages pulled by pairs of white horses. 'Close beside the platform we were shown into a very comfortable suite of rooms, with beds prepared ready for us – Her Highness's own private waiting rooms, the place where she had conversed with Lord Curzon for two hours – at our disposal until the train for Bombay would leave at about 2.30 a.m.'

Captain Ahmed made Lilah write her address in his pocket book. He wanted to send her photographs. On the dark platform he looked directly into her eyes on the dark platform; he would call her in London later in the year; he would give her lessons in Hindustani if she would give him lessons in English – 'but now we must part,' he said "parting is such sweet sorrow". The message was clear.

As they waited for the night train on their wooden beds, Lilah confided in Sylvia that her romantic feelings had been engaged as never before. Sylvia was robust: 'she told me I was infatuated with India and the stars and the moon on the Prince's lakes and the "magic of the East", not with Capt Ahmed. I could not help thinking that that was just what I had said to Gerald!' Even so 'he was awfully good looking and I had watched him go with such regret as he had been so terribly kind and had seemed to look right into my soul when we talked...'

19

Voyage Home

For the first and only time in Lilah's two-month journey, Arthur Brodrick's normally impeccable arrangements proved too demanding. Soon after reaching Bangalore she succumbed to exhaustion. The Garden City, as it was called, was the centre of colonial rule in South India, an expatriate utopia, with its clubs, its cricket, its pretty bungalows, its abundant bougainvillea and its immaculate polo ground, where on its surface like a billiard table officers played as hard as they drank. Lilah was far from immune to its charms, but it was not what she had come to India for – or rather not what she had come to love about India. Maybe her tiredness was an escape from being paired off by the British memsahibs with yet another eligible army officer, Major Dalgety. Maybe she was nostalgic for Bhopal. More probably she was simply dreading going home and grieving that her inseparable ally Sylvia had left her to prolong her own stay until the autumn. Whatever the cause, Lilah retired to her bed for several days, fighting the temptation to change her mind and accept the invitations she had refused. But she had neither the money nor the will to defy her mother. She must return. With Lilah confined to her room, Arthur delayed the journey south and shortened to two days their visit to Ceylon.

On 1 February 1912 a small rowing boat ferried her, together with Judy and Arthur Brodrick, out of Colombo to the P&O steamship *Malwa*. Lilah bade a private last farewell of Ceylon and India and 'set her face homewards'. The *Malwa* was 2,000 tons smaller than the *Maloja*. On board were a handful of English and many Australians, nearly all of them much older than Lilah. Despondent without Sylvia, her spirits dropped further as she unpacked in her cabin. It was not so much the lack of company as the thought of her duties towards her mother and above all an intense sense of loss – not so much of Captain Ahmed as of the whole Indian experience which he embodied, and which had reawakened the confidence and adventurousness of her Irish youth. 'It is so strange and sad and difficult to have left it all behind me.'

Two English passengers with animals provided a tangible link with the India she was leaving. Mrs Fitzroy's tame sparrowhawk, given her by 'some prince or other', was an object of fascination 'She walks about with it sitting on her wrist – it has the most lovely yellow eyes ... she brings it each day on deck to sun itself and get some air ... He succeeds in scratching my finger with one of his claws rather badly when I have him on my wrist.'

Alice Teck, too, was a consolation. Pretty and vivacious and the same age as Lilah, she made as good a substitute for Sylvia as Lilah could have hoped for. She kept two green parakeets she had bought in India in her cabin, which was next to Lilah's. Close up the birds were surprisingly ugly, with narrow wings, desperately darting about like green arrows. From time to time there would be a great hue and cry when they escaped. An hour or two later they would be found sitting quietly by their cage in the Tecks' cabin. Lilah and Alice took to reminiscing. Alice had collected piles of official photographs, but they were too formal to evoke personal memories and Lilah preferred it when she laid out on her bed, like a bazaar merchant, the jewels and precious stones she had amassed in India 'especially a most lovely rope of pearls'.

Lilah was not so dejected as to have lost her curiosity: 'A flying fish flew in at the porthole of a lady's maid's cabin last night and gave her quite a fright till she saw what it was that flopped about on her bed! She kept it to show us this morning – it was a pretty beast, with silvery white scales and blue wings.' Two days later she noted: 'There is a luminous phosphorescence at night on the sea surface ... The Southern Cross is visible now in the sky at about 3 in the morning ... just four very brilliant stars but this is the only place in the world where it is to be seen.'

Events on board did nothing to relieve her mood. Morbid superstition was in the air. 'Mrs Fitzroy feels poorly. She is in a great fright about herself, as she was in the room next to a man who developed cholera in a hotel she stayed in at Madras and she wonders if she will get it too.' Just before they reached Aden someone actually died. One of the second class passengers succumbed to consumption and was buried at sea the same morning. 'The bell tolled throughout the ship. While the service was being read, the body, covered with the Union Jack, was lowered into the sea. All the passengers attending cried and even some of the ship's officers and stewards. It seemed so tragic and sudden as he was sitting on deck on Sunday and now he was buried on Wednesday morning but I suppose a quick burial is necessary in this climate. ... He had no one on board belonging to him, but he has a wife and family in England.'

Worse was to come, with the news that Alice's uncle by marriage, the Duke of Fife, had died in Egypt. 'His body has been taken on from Port Sudan by another ship. We thought for a while it might fall to the lot of our boat to convey the corpse home and none of us liked the idea. We felt it might curse our voyage.' Court etiquette required Alice to go into mourning. 'I see little of her now, she is in black and cannot be social, much as she would like to go dancing at night. His death was very tragic, the Duchess being all alone with him in Egypt and coming on top of the awful shipwreck they went through the other day.' Time passed slower and slower.

There were, of course, the customary ship flirtations, but for Lilah this sport had lost all interest. The Captain had taken a shine to her, inviting her on long strolls round the deck before dinner, telling her stories, showing her photographs and taking her aloft to show her how the wireless telegraphy worked. One Australian was very persistent and 'far too forward'. And then there was the purser. A tall and very good-looking man, he took her for walks on the lower deck, an infallible pretext for the English passengers on the upper deck to tease her. Admiral Colville composed a poem during dinner and sent it by one of the stewards to Lilah's table. Believing she must play the game, and wanting to hide her dejection, she winged back a poem in reply. In deepening gloom, that night she wrote: 'The East is all behind me ... except for the glimpses I shall see at Aden and Port Said – it is all a thing of the past, I shall not see India any more.'

Alone in her cabin, she began to sift through her own photographs. Would they unlock something, give meaning to the clues that eluded her? Nothing in India was definable. '...the force behind the colour and the movement, crowds in the bazaar, the rainbow of draperies, the brown bodies, ringed native women, their teeth and lips red from chewing

Peshawar: Lilah stays with the High Commisioner for a week in December 1911

The bodyguard assigned to Lilah for her
protection during her stay in Peshawar

Lilah sets off early for the Khyber Pass
in a tonga behind her friends

Lilah (sitting second left) on the Khyber Pass at the furthermost border of the British frontier with armed escort

Lilah and Judy Smith take a break on the Khyber Pass

Lilah outside Lady Helen Mitford's bungalow at Rawalpindi

Major Gosling preparing the boat for Lilah to go up the Ganges

Hindu cremation: the body is laid out before being set alight

Lilah (right) and Judy Smith suck sugar cane at a police station outside Agra

Lilah's first sight of the Taj Mahal

The Maharana of Udaipur who left early
during the Delhi Durbar

The Maharaja of Jaipur's elephant which he
lent to Lilah

Prince Obaidullah, the Begum of Bhopal's son, takes Lilah to an island for a picnic

Snipe shooting during the picnic

Captain Amir Ahmed

Lilah in Colombo before catching the ship home

On board the *Malwa*, Alice Teck (left),
Mrs Fitzroy and Lady Adelaide Colville

Mrs Fitzroy with her Indian bird

The Theosophist Annie Besant arriving in
London with Krishnamurti (right)

Lilah's disapproving mother

Lilah met Clive Morrison-Bell straight after her return to London from India. Within the
month they were engaged.

betel-nut, the "dirgie" cross-legged on the verandah mending one's clothes, the glorious sunsets, the pageantry of birds and strings of gentle buffalo, laden with sugarcane, trailing clouds of dust and baggy-trousered Pathans astride upon their haunches, water bottles bobbing at their sides...' How was she to order and digest all these impressions?

At Aden Lilah's depression and detachment at last began to lift. Forty new passengers came aboard, having transferred from the *Salsette,* which had come from Bombay. Three appeared interesting: a young nephew of Sir Patrap Singh; a strong-looking old man with a striking resemblance to Gladstone, who turned out to be his son; and an elderly woman with a majestic presence and a firm, beautiful face and short white curly hair. She arrived on deck with no hat in a long white garment, accompanied by two Indian boys.

Arthur Brodrick knew all about Annie Besant. He remembered hearing of a court case connected to her past. In her youth she had married a clergyman, but had been ordered to leave his house when, having embraced atheism, she refused Communion. During the years that followed she had written articles on marriage and women's rights and had become a leading advocate of birth control. The provocative material she published was deemed by the law courts 'likely to deprave or corrupt those whose minds are open to moral influence'. She was charged in 1877 and found guilty. Amid a public uproar, the sentence was quashed on appeal.

Annie Besant was also famous for being the President of the Theosophical Society. Theosophy was an esoteric religion founded by a Madame Blavatsky. Lilah was intrigued. 'The two Hindu boys on board with her are disciples of hers and one of them she believes to be a sort of Mohammed or some wonderful reincarnation who is going to do great things. I should love to hear her views.'

Next morning, Lilah and Annie Besant passed each other in the passage. Lilah introduced herself. They recognised inflections of a shared Irish background. Annie's generous response to Lilah's faltering conversation left her captivated by her 'supernatural psychic energy'. The two sat on deck together. That night Lilah wrote in her diary:

She has been living at Adyar in Madras, teaching in a college at Benares, the holy city of the Hindus. To her, Hinduism is the highest form of all existing faiths. Theosophy was based on Hindu ideas of karma and reincarnation with nirvana as the eventual aim. Most Theosophists believe that every two thousand years or so a superhuman being called the Lord Maitreya, the World Teacher, comes to earth to occupy a human body and found a new religion to help humanity along the path of evolution. The bodies of Shri Krishna and Christ had both been used in this way. Annie believes it is now almost time for the Lord Maitreya to come again, she already knew whose body he was to occupy – it is not the beautiful Indian boy, Nitya, with her but the older one, Krishna, always dreamy and quiet.

Day by day Annie continued to exert her magnetism on Lilah, explaining how India had transformed her religious understanding. Lilah was far too enthralled to feel she was being lectured. 'Truth,' Annie told her, 'can be found in all religions. We do not shut out anyone because he does not believe in theosophical teachings. A man may deny every one of the great religions, except that of human brotherhood, and claim his rightful place amongst our ranks.'

As she became more immersed in Annie and her two Indians, Lilah's zest for life returned. Together with Krishna and Nitya she watched and fed Mrs Fitzroy's birds. Both boys had a special aura about them, Nitya so full of life, his older brother Krishna so full of dreams. Arthur Brodrick warned her that Annie Besant's guardianship over the boys was in jeopardy. The Madras newspapers had reported that their father, a long-standing Theosophist, had dispensed with his sense of brother-hood to file a lawsuit to recover custody of his sons. Annie had all but abducted them and secretly booked the passage on this ship a week earlier than she had declared.

On the spur of the moment, and out of concern for her friend, Mrs Fitzroy suggested she and Lilah escape the ship at Suez for the twenty-four hours allotted before it was due to leave from Port Said, at the other end of the Suez Canal. They would visit the Great Pyramids. Lilah immediately agreed. Besides the adventure, a respite from the intensity of Annie's companionship might be no bad thing.

Once on land, they found a train to Cairo, where they would stop overnight. They felt a twinge of anxiety as they watched the *Malwa* in the distance, steaming away up the Canal. Disappointed at seeing nothing of Egypt during the night journey, they reached Cairo before midnight and boarded a coach which took them at a terrific pace through the main streets and out onto a straight road bordered by trees. After eight miles they came to the Mena House Hotel, where they shared a room to save expense.

> Before going to bed we looked out of our window and saw the huge pyramids black and massive against the star-lit sky – quite close to the hotel, beyond them the desert, silent and ghostly and immeasurably vast... We got up at 5.30 a.m. – a bitter cold dark morning – and were supplied with no hot water to wash in and no tea to support us, but we dressed and went straight out, mounted two donkeys which with their attendant Arab boys awaited us by order of the night before and rode out to see the sun rise over the Pyramids. I have seldom seen anything so beautiful, the darkness changing to a vivid pink glow and then to orange and crimson and later to a pearly blue – a glorious background to the immense blocks of stone and the Sphinx, the oldest known monument in the world, which stood out lonely and contemptuous close by the ruins of the temple of the Sphinx, with its huge solid pillars of grey stone and pinky granite. And beyond all lay the desert, with its delicate yellow tones of colour, all misty in the early dawn. Not a living soul but our two selves and our donkey boys. Far away was a green oasis of palm trees where a strip of blue water showed dimly and a few solitary Arabs with their camels rested – a speck of dark in the colour scheme of yellow and rose.

They went a little way up one of the narrow winding passages inside a pyramid but, in Lilah's words, had 'no time to do more than take a look round, rushing back to the hotel for breakfast, motor back to Cairo through the bazaars and visit one mosque and the Citadel and then to the station to catch our train. It was all a great rush of course and only having had four hours' sleep I was pretty done.'

But it had been well worth it and they saw a good deal more of the desert, the Nile and the Suez Canal from the windows of the train as they dozed their way north to Port Said. They boarded the ship again at four o'clock and she left Port Said at five.

After dinner that night Lilah walked round the deck talking with Annie, who explained details of the new society she had founded, called the Order of the Star in the East, with the sixteen-year-old Jiddu Krishnamurti as its head: his body had been chosen by the Lord Maitreya to be the vehicle for the new Messiah. He had already had one initiation and she was taking him to Sicily for further training.

Just before the end of the voyage, Annie took Lilah further into her confidence. She was intending to relinquish her leadership of the Theosophist movement to take on Indian Home Rule. She would be handing over her work to another colleague as Indian Liberation was of vital importance to the Masters. Lilah was dumbstruck. She had had no idea that Annie was involved with Indian nationalism.

They arrived into London in the grey, bleak fog of a February morning, stepping onto the platform to a flash of photographers. Surrounded by journalists Annie could only wave goodbye to Lilah. Within half an hour Lilah had reached Harley Street to find her mother waiting for her in the sitting room.

20

Epilogue

In February 1912 the London papers were full of the King's visit, embellishing India's exotic image with romantic jingoism. The Durbar film showed to long queues in Piccadilly. A full-page picture of Lilah appeared in *The Lady*, dressed in her Irish fancy dress costume. Hostesses were hungry for her first-hand account. Her dramatic story-telling engendered much gossip and amusement, but her odyssey was also seen as a courageous adventure and a welcome distraction from the tense political situation at home, where industrial unrest was rife and the atmosphere in Westminster highly charged. Two general elections in 1910 had left Parliament in a dangerous mood. Scenes of uncontrollable anger were continually breaking out over the campaign for Irish independence and the Lords' right to veto Commons legislation. Prime Minister Asquith had been howled down with cries of 'traitor'. On one occasion the House had had to be adjourned.

Amid this turmoil, a Conservative MP, Clive Morrison-Bell, met Lilah at a mutual friend's invitation in the spring of 1912. He recalled in his memoirs: 'I suddenly fell violently in love with a young lady that I met one evening at a dinner party – all my concerns could go to the bottom of the sea for all I cared.' He cancelled everything and telegraphed her that he was on his way to Dublin. Could he come to Powerscourt for lunch? He packed, left for Euston station and caught the night train to Holyhead. By the end of the year he and Lilah were married.

As for India, would the King's visit reverse the tide of nationalism? If so, would the effect be lasting? Lilah had witnessed the astonishing loyalty that had swept over the country during the Durbar. With his deep respect for the maharajas, the King had soothed sensibilities bruised by the Colonial Government's high-handedness, reaffirming Britain's promises in the most uncompromising words: 'ever to maintain the privileges, rights and dignities of the Indian Princes, who may rest assured that this pledge is inviolate and inviolable'.

On the day of the King's return to London, the Princes communicated to the Prime Minister their own pledge, their indissolubly linked destiny and their loyal and loving homage to the Crown. The King's historic visit, they wrote, marked the beginning of a new era. India was proud of her place in the Empire. To prove herself worthy of it she would seek to quell internal animosities and would freely cooperate with England in working out her future. With patience the British could eventually hand over through the Princes a devolved power structure, in which democracy and the rule of law would be firmly entrenched.

But the real question was whether the Princes still held the key to India's future. Lilah's conversations with Colonel Barnes and Annie Besant had sown seeds of doubt in her mind. The power of the maharajas was tied up with the power of the Raj, but significant numbers of Indians, particularly among the rising middle class, resented their colonial status. And great changes were coming. In 1915 Gandhi would return from South Africa to campaign for the removal of foreign powers from India. The First World War was two years away, the Russian Revolution five, and with them the overthrow of every European empire except the British. The massacre at Amritsar in 1919 would leave an indelible stain on the Raj.

Lilah watched from afar the fortunes of those she had encountered on her journeys through India. The Military Command had been right to be concerned for Lord Hardinge's safety. One year after the Durbar, leading the Viceregal Entry into Delhi on an elephant to mark the transfer of the capital from Calcutta, he was targeted by a homemade bomb and severely wounded. His bodyguard took the brunt of the explosion and was killed. Lady Hardinge, seated on the howdah beside her husband, never recovered from the shock and died prematurely two years later.

After this attack, Hardinge's distrust of progressive Indians intensified. In 1913 he ordered the chief of the CID to impose a special watch on the Gaekwar of Baroda and persuaded the King not to receive him. But Viceroys come and Viceroys go. King George forgave the Gaekwar in 1917 and honoured him with a high decoration. The Maharana of Mewar, however, who had declined outright to attend the Durbar ceremony, had no reprieve. Deemed 'inflexible and ignorant' at a time of social unrest in his state, he was deposed and replaced by his son.

Lilah's instincts about the Maharaja of Indore had been sound. In 1925 he was implicated in a scandalous murder after one of his harem escaped from his private train and fled to Bombay. Ordered to capture her, his hired henchmen slashed the concubine's face and stabbed her protector to death. The leading maharajas had the right to be tried by their peers, but rather than risk the possible embarrassment of an inconclusive trial, the Government forced him to abdicate.

As for the Begum of Bhopal, Amir Ahmed's forebodings had been right. After a decade of family squabbles over succession, she abdicated sadly in 1926 in favour of her third son, bringing an end to more than a hundred years of female rule. She died four years later, aged seventy-one.

Many of the maharajas provided troops, support and money, and even volunteered to fight to help the Allies in the First World War. Under Sir Pratap Singh's influence, the young Maharaja of Jodhpur, Sumer, joined his Regent at the front, fought for a short while but soon returned to his state, went the dissolute way of his father and died at the age of twenty. Sir P himself fought with outstanding courage as a seventy-year-old, commanding his regiments in France, Flanders and the Middle East. He was promoted to lieutenant-general in 1916. When Sumer's brother, Maharaja Umaid (the present Maharaja's grandfather), became the Ruler in 1918 he learned everything he could from Sir P, who yet again became Regent. Third time lucky, this time his charge was exceptional and he went on to be remembered as the builder of modern Jodhpur.

The First World War took a heavy toll of the 10th Hussars. Gerald Stewart was to die in 1915 in the Second Battle of Ypres, alongside four other Hussar officers, including Major Mitford. Colonel Barnes was twice wounded, four times mentioned in dispatches and awarded the Croix de Guerre. He was promoted to brigadier general and knighted. In 1919 he married a Dutch widow. Basil Brooke survived the war with a shattered jaw. He won the Military Cross and the Croix de Guerre, and in 1920 left the Army to become a politician, later serving as Prime Minister of Northern Ireland for almost twenty years.

Basil's sister, Lilah's beloved friend Sylvia Brooke, married Charles Mulholland in 1920, but died in childbirth the following year Her husband remarried and in 1931 inherited the barony of Dunleath.

Before returning from India Sylvia wrote to Lilah that she had told Amir Ahmed of Lilah's engagement to Clive. The Captain immediately dropped their correspondence and never made contact again.

The ships also had a bad end. The *Medina* sank in 1917, torpedoed by a U-boat off the coast of Devon. The *Maloja* struck a mine two miles off Dover in 1916 and sank.

In her old age, Lilah moved permanently to Norfolk. In 1974 a fire devoured and gutted Powerscourt Castle and she never returned to Ireland. Nor did she return to India. She kept to the end the memories of India's radiance, its strong perfumes, market places, birds, horses, camels, monkeys and elephants – and of a land of tradition, tribe and caste, of landowners and princely states, of antiquity and anachronism, hierarchy and honour, order and subordination, glory and chivalry.

With the coming of democracy, the maharajas Lilah admired, who once ruled a third of India's people, faded so completely from the scene that their days of glory soon seemed as distant as those of the Mughals. Their palaces became museums, schools or hotels. Yet the experience of what India once was remained in Lilah's heart, stripped of all flaws by the perfecting influence of nostalgia.

She did not pass her time in India with famous people, nor did she see the country with a historian's eyes. Her diary was written for herself, not for posterity. That is what gives it its authenticity and its absence of pretence or pretentiousness. I have called the book 'A Glimpse of Empire', which it is. It is also a glimpse of an England that no longer exists, but that once inspired a million soldiers to lay down their lives for it.

Index

horseriding, 53–4, 82, 108; dances with Gerald Stewart, 55, 70; turns down Colonel Barnes, 56, 68–9, 82–3; attends garden party at Red Fort, 64; watches King's military review, 69; acquires jewels, 71, 94, 115; leaves for Peshawar and North-West Frontier, 72, 75–7; attitude to India and Indians, 73, 77, 114–16, 124; in Rawalpindi, 83; travels in northern India, 83–113; eats Indian food, 91; rides elephant, 95–6; in Bhopal, 100–11; falls for Captain Ahmed, 113, 114; exhaustion on trip to south India and Ceylon, 114; on return voyage to England, 114–15; marriage, 121; pictured in *The Lady*, 121; moves to Norfolk, 124

Wingfield, Maurice (Lilah's uncle), 4
Wingfield, Mervyn (Lilah's brother) *see* Powerscourt, 8th Viscount
Wingfield, Olive (*later* Van de Weyer; Lilah's sister), 5, 19
Wyllie, Sir Curzon, 13